English/Chinese Edition

The New Oxford Picture Dictionary

E.C. Parnwell

Translated by Hsiao-yiing Liu

Illustrations by:
Ray Burns
Bob Giuliani
Laura Hartman
Pamela Johnson
Melodye Rosales
Raymond Skibinski
Joel Snyder

Oxford University Press

Oxford University Press

198 Madison Avenue
New York, NY 10016 USA

Great Clarendon Street
Oxford OX2 6DP England

Oxford New York
Athens Auckland Bangkok Bogotá Buenos Aires
Calcutta Cape Town Chennai Dar es Salaam
Delhi Florence Hong Kong Istanbul Karachi
Kuala Lumpur Madrid Melbourne Mexico City
Mumbai Nairobi Paris São Paulo Shanghai
Singapore Taipei Tokyo Toronto Warsaw

and associated companies in
Berlin Ibadan

OXFORD is a trademark of Oxford University Press.

ISBN 0-19-434357-X

Copyright © 1989 by Oxford University Press

Developmental Editor: Margot Gramer
Associate Editor: Mary Lynne Nielsen
Art Director: Lynn Luchetti
Production Co-ordinator: Claire Nicholl
The publishers would like to thank the following agents for their co-operation:
Carol Bancroft and Friends, representing Bob Giuliani,
Laura Hartman, and Melodye Rosales.

Publishers Graphics Inc., representing Ray Burns,
Pamela Johnson, and Joel Snyder.

Cover illustration by Laura Hartman.

Printing (last digit): 15 14 13

Printed in China

The New Oxford Picture Dictionary contextually illustrates over 2,400 words. The book is a unique language learning tool for students of English. It provides students with a glance at American lifestyle, as well as a compendium of useful vocabulary.

The *Dictionary* is organized thematically, beginning with topics that are most useful for the "survival" needs of students in an English-speaking country. However, pages may be used at random, depending on the students' particular needs. The book need not be taught in order. A complete index with pronunciation guide in English is in the Appendix.

The New Oxford Picture Dictionary contextualizes vocabulary whenever possible. Verbs have been included on separate pages, but within a topic area where they are most likely to occur. However, this does not imply that these verbs only appear within these contexts.

For further ideas using *The New Oxford Picture Dictionary*, see the *Listening and Speaking Activity Book*, the *Teacher's Guide*, and the two workbooks: *Beginner's* and *Intermediate* levels. Also available in the program are a complete set of *Cassettes*, offering a reading of all of the words in the *Dictionary; Vocabulary Playing Cards*, featuring 40 words and the corresponding pictures on 80 cards, with ideas for many games; and sets of *Wall Charts*, available in one complete package or in three smaller packages. All of these items are available in English only.

前　言

　　《新牛津圖解字典》分門別類列出二千四百多個詞彙。這本字典是學習英語的獨特工具，當中不僅有許多實用單字，還粗略地介紹了美國生活方式。

　　這本字典按照主題編排，從學生在英語國家生活中最迫切需要的入手。不過，這本書不必按次序教授，可以根據學生的特別需要而選擇使用。附錄是一份完整的發音索引。

　　《新牛津圖解字典》盡可能分門別類列舉詞彙。這些詞彙當中包括了某些主題常用的動詞。雖然這些動詞列於特定主題，但這並不表示這些動詞不能用於其他主題。

　　若讀者想進一步了解如何使用這本字典，請參閱《教師指南》和兩本練習用書（初學者和中等程度用書）。我們還有一套完整的錄音帶，單字遊戲卡和掛圖。錄音帶中有本字典所有的單字發音。單字卡收入四十個詞彙和四十張配合的圖片，可用來玩許多遊戲。掛圖分爲一套整裝及三套分裝形式。除了《新牛津圖解字典》是英漢對照外，其他輔助教材都是英文版。

People and Relationships   人物及其關係   *Page*   2
The Family   家庭   3
The Human Body   人體   4–5
Vegetables   蔬菜   6–7
Fruits   水果   8–9
Meat, Poultry, and Seafood   肉類，家禽及海產   10–11
Containers, Quantities, and Money   容器，量及錢幣   12–13
The Supermarket   超級市場   14–15
Family Restaurant and Cocktail Lounge   家庭餐館及酒吧   16
Restaurant Verbs   餐館用詞(動詞)   17
Common Prepared Foods   家常食物   18
Outdoor Clothes   戶外服裝   19
Everyday Clothes   日常服裝   20–21
Underwear and Sleepwear   內衣及睡衣   22
Jewelry and Cosmetics   珠寶及化粧品   23
Describing Clothes   描述服裝   24
Describing the Weather   描述天氣   25
Seasonal Verbs   季節用詞(動詞)   26
Houses   房子   27
The Living Room   起居室   28
The Dining Room   飯廳   29
The Kitchen   廚房   30
Kitchen Verbs   廚房用詞(動詞)   31
The Bedroom   臥房   32
The Baby's Room   嬰兒房   33
The Bathroom   浴室   34
The Utility Room   工作房   35
A Workshop   工作間   36–37
Housework and Repair Verbs   家事及修理用詞(動詞)   38
Medical and Dental Care   醫療及牙齒保健   39
Ailments and Injuries   疾病及損傷   40
Treatments and Remedies   治療   41
Firefighting and Rescue   救火及援救   42
Crime and Punishment   犯罪及懲罰   43
The City   城市   44–45
The U.S. Postal System   美國郵政系統   46
The Public Library   公立圖書館   47
The Armed Forces   武裝力量   48
Trucks   卡車   49
Cars   轎車   50–51
Bikes   自行車   52
Highway Travel   高速公路旅行   53
Public Transportation   公共交通運輸   54–55
Air Travel   航空旅行   56
Aircraft   航空器   57
In Port   在港口   58
Pleasure Boating   遊船   59
Plants and Trees   植物及樹木   60–61
Simple Animals   低等動物   62
Insects   昆蟲   63
Birds   鳥類   64
Fish and Reptiles   魚類及爬蟲類   65

Mammals I　哺乳類一　　　　　　　　　　　　　　*Page*　66–67
Mammals II　哺乳類二　　　　　　　　　　　　　　68–69
Map of the World　世界地圖　　　　　　　　　　　70–71
The United States of America　美國　　　　　　　72–73
The Universe　宇宙　　　　　　　　　　　　　　74
The Space Program　航天計劃　　　　　　　　　　75
A Classroom　教室　　　　　　　　　　　　　　76
School Verbs　學校用詞(動詞)　　　　　　　　　77
A Science Lab　科學實驗室　　　　　　　　　　78
Math　數學　　　　　　　　　　　　　　　　　79
Energy　能量　　　　　　　　　　　　　　　　80
Farming and Ranching　農作及畜牧　　　　　　　81
Construction　建築　　　　　　　　　　　　　　82
An Office　辦公室　　　　　　　　　　　　　　83
Occupations I: Main Street USA　職業一：美國大街　84
Occupations II　職業二　　　　　　　　　　　　85
Occupations III　職業三　　　　　　　　　　　　86
Neighborhood Parks　鄰近公園　　　　　　　　　87
Outdoor Activities　戶外活動　　　　　　　　　88–89
At the Beach　在海灘　　　　　　　　　　　　　90–91
Team Sports　球隊運動　　　　　　　　　　　　92
Ballfields　球場　　　　　　　　　　　　　　　93
Individual Sports　個人運動　　　　　　　　　　94
Fields and Courses　球場及跑道　　　　　　　　95
Sports Verbs　運動用詞(動詞)　　　　　　　　96–97
Musical Instruments　樂器　　　　　　　　　　　98
Music, Dance, and Theater　音樂、舞蹈及劇院　　99
Electronics and Photography　電子及攝影器材　　100
Handicrafts　手工藝　　　　　　　　　　　　　101
Prepositions of Description　描述用詞(介系詞)　102
Prepositions of Motion　動作用詞(介系詞)　　　103
Appendix　附錄　　　　　　　　　　　　　　　104
Index　索引　　　　　　　　　　　　　　　　　105

女人	**1.** woman	孩子	**7.** children
男人	**2.** man	男孩	**8.** boy
丈夫	**3.** husband	女孩	**9.** girl
妻子	**4.** wife	祖父母、外祖父母	**10.** grandparents
嬰兒，嬰孩	**5.** baby	孫女，外孫女	**11.** granddaughter
父母	**6.** parents	孫子，外孫	**12.** grandson

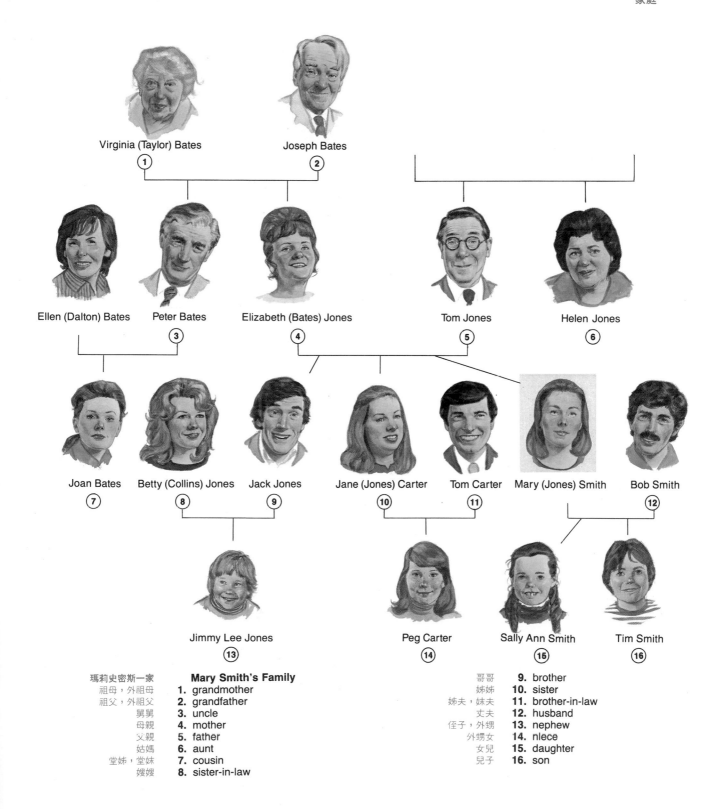

Virginia (Taylor) Bates ①
Joseph Bates ②
Ellen (Dalton) Bates ③
Peter Bates
Elizabeth (Bates) Jones ④
Tom Jones ⑤
Helen Jones ⑥
Joan Bates ⑦
Betty (Collins) Jones ⑧
Jack Jones ⑨
Jane (Jones) Carter ⑩
Tom Carter ⑪
Mary (Jones) Smith
Bob Smith ⑫
Jimmy Lee Jones ⑬
Peg Carter ⑭
Sally Ann Smith ⑮
Tim Smith ⑯

瑪莉史密斯一家　　**Mary Smith's Family**
祖母，外祖母　**1.** grandmother
祖父，外祖父　**2.** grandfather
舅舅　**3.** uncle
母親　**4.** mother
父親　**5.** father
姑媽　**6.** aunt
堂姊，堂妹　**7.** cousin
嫂嫂　**8.** sister-in-law

哥哥　**9.** brother
姊姊　**10.** sister
姊夫，妹夫　**11.** brother-in-law
丈夫　**12.** husband
侄子，外甥　**13.** nephew
外甥女　**14.** niece
女兒　**15.** daughter
兒子　**16.** son

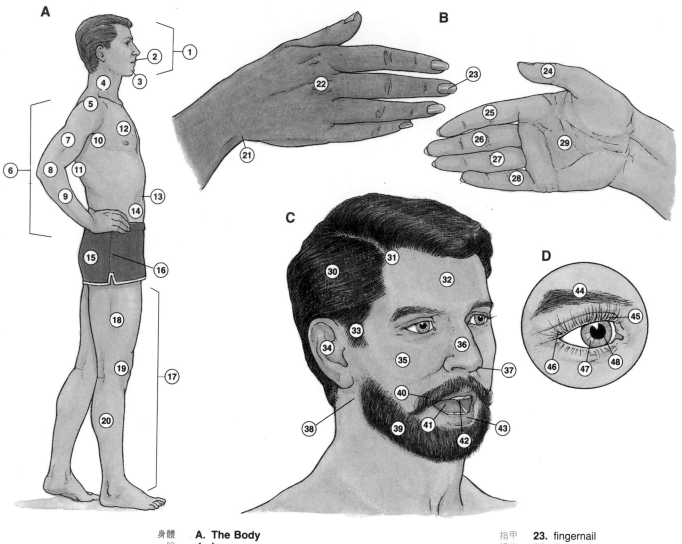

身體	**A.**	**The Body**
臉	**1.**	face
口，嘴	**2.**	mouth
下巴	**3.**	chin
脖子	**4.**	neck
肩膀	**5.**	shoulder
手臂	**6.**	arm
上臂	**7.**	upper arm
肘	**8.**	elbow
前臂	**9.**	forearm
腋下，腋窩	**10.**	armpit
背	**11.**	back
胸	**12.**	chest
腰	**13.**	waist
腹	**14.**	abdomen
臀部	**15.**	buttocks
臀，股	**16.**	hip
腿	**17.**	leg
大腿	**18.**	thigh
膝	**19.**	knee
小腿	**20.**	calf
手	**B.**	**The Hand**
手腕	**21.**	wrist
指關節	**22.**	knuckle

指甲	**23.**	fingernail
拇指	**24.**	thumb
食指	**25.**	(index) finger
中指	**26.**	middle finger
無名指	**27.**	ring finger
小指	**28.**	little finger
手掌	**29.**	palm
頭	**C.**	**The Head**
頭髮	**30.**	hair
分髮線	**31.**	part
額	**32.**	forehead
鬢腳	**33.**	sideburn
耳	**34.**	ear
臉頰	**35.**	cheek
鼻子	**36.**	nose
鼻孔	**37.**	nostril
下顎	**38.**	jaw
鬍子	**39.**	beard
髭	**40.**	mustache
舌	**41.**	tongue
牙	**42.**	tooth
唇	**43.**	lip

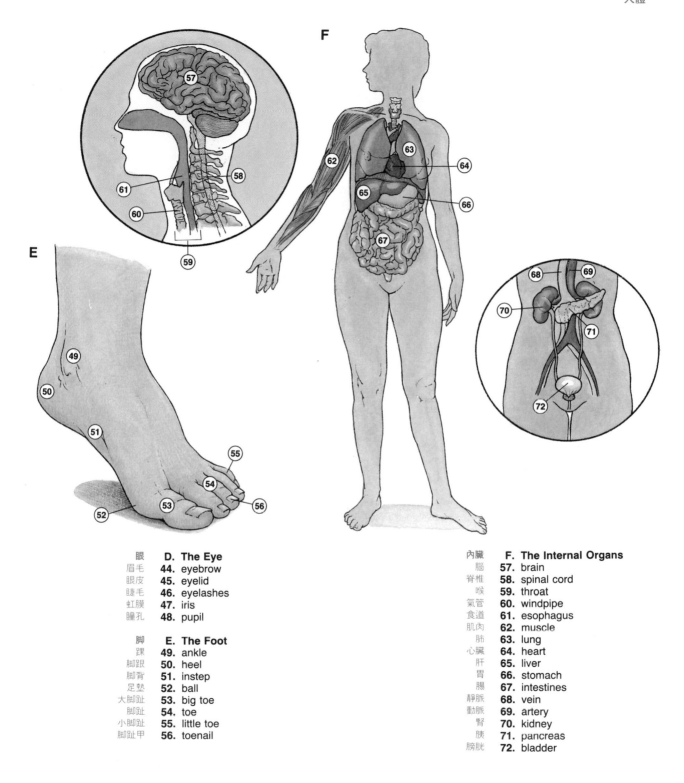

E

F

眼	D. The Eye
眉毛	44. eyebrow
眼皮	45. eyelid
睫毛	46. eyelashes
虹膜	47. iris
瞳孔	48. pupil

脚	E. The Foot
踝	49. ankle
脚跟	50. heel
脚背	51. instep
足墊	52. ball
大脚趾	53. big toe
脚趾	54. toe
小脚趾	55. little toe
脚趾甲	56. toenail

內臟	F. The Internal Organs
腦	57. brain
脊椎	58. spinal cord
喉	59. throat
氣管	60. windpipe
食道	61. esophagus
肌肉	62. muscle
肺	63. lung
心臟	64. heart
肝	65. liver
胃	66. stomach
腸	67. intestines
靜脈	68. vein
動脈	69. artery
腎	70. kidney
胰	71. pancreas
膀胱	72. bladder

花椰菜（結球）	**1.** (head of) cauliflower	朝鮮薊	**11.** artichoke
芥蘭菜	**2.** broccoli	玉蜀黍，玉米（穗）	**12.** (ear of) corn
捲心菜	**3.** cabbage	玉米穗軸	**a.** cob
芽甘藍	**4.** brussels sprouts	菜豆	**13.** kidney bean(s)
水芥菜	**5.** watercress	黑豆	**14.** black bean(s)
萵苣菜	**6.** lettuce	四季豆，刀豆	**15.** string bean(s)
生菜	**7.** escarole	青豆，利馬豆	**16.** lima bean(s)
菠菜	**8.** spinach	碗豆	**17.** pea(s)
藥草	**9.** herb(s)	莢	**a.** pod
芹菜	**10.** celery	蘆筍	**18.** asparagus

蕃茄，西紅柿	**19.** tomato(es)
黃瓜	**20.** cucumber(s)
茄子	**21.** eggplant
青椒	**22.** pepper(s)
馬鈴薯，土豆	**23.** potato(es)
甘薯	**24.** yam
大蒜	**25.** garlic
鱗莖，珠芽	**a.** clove
南瓜	**26.** pumpkin

祖齊瓜	**27.** zucchini
橡形南瓜	**28.** acorn squash
辣根	**29.** radish(es)
磨菇	**30.** mushroom(s)
洋葱	**31.** onion(s)
胡蘿蔔	**32.** carrot(s)
甜菜	**33.** beet(s)
蕪菁	**34.** turnip

(一串)葡萄	**1.** (a bunch of) grapes		檸檬	**9.** lemon
蘋果	**2.** apple		萊姆果	**10.** lime
果柄	**a.** stem			
果心	**b.** core		**漿果類**	**Berries**
椰子	**3.** coconut		醋栗果	**11.** gooseberries
菠蘿，鳳梨	**4.** pineapple		黑莓	**12.** blackberries
芒果	**5.** mango		蔓越橘	**13.** cranberries
木瓜	**6.** papaya		都柿果	**14.** blueberries
			草莓	**15.** strawberry
			覆盆子	**16.** raspberries
柑橘類水果	**Citrus Fruits**			
葡萄柚	**7.** grapefruit		油桃	**17.** nectarine
橙子	**8.** orange		梨子	**18.** pear
片	**a.** section			
皮	**b.** rind			
籽	**c.** seed			

櫻桃	**19.** cherries	堅果	**Nuts**
（一掛）香蕉	**20.** (a bunch of) bananas	槽如果	**27.** cashew(s)
香蕉皮	**a.** peel	花生	**28.** peanut(s)
		核桃	**29.** walnut(s)
乾果類	**Dried Fruits**	榛實	**30.** hazelnut(s)
無花果	**21.** fig	杏仁	**31.** almond(s)
乾梅	**22.** prune	栗子	**32.** chestnut(s)
棗椰	**23.** date		
葡萄乾	**24.** raisin(s)	鱷梨	**33.** avocado
		李子	**34.** plum
杏子	**25.** apricot	蜜瓜	**35.** honeydew melon
西瓜	**26.** watermelon	小甜瓜	**36.** cantaloupe
		桃子	**37.** peach
		桃核	**a.** pit
		桃皮	**b.** skin

A

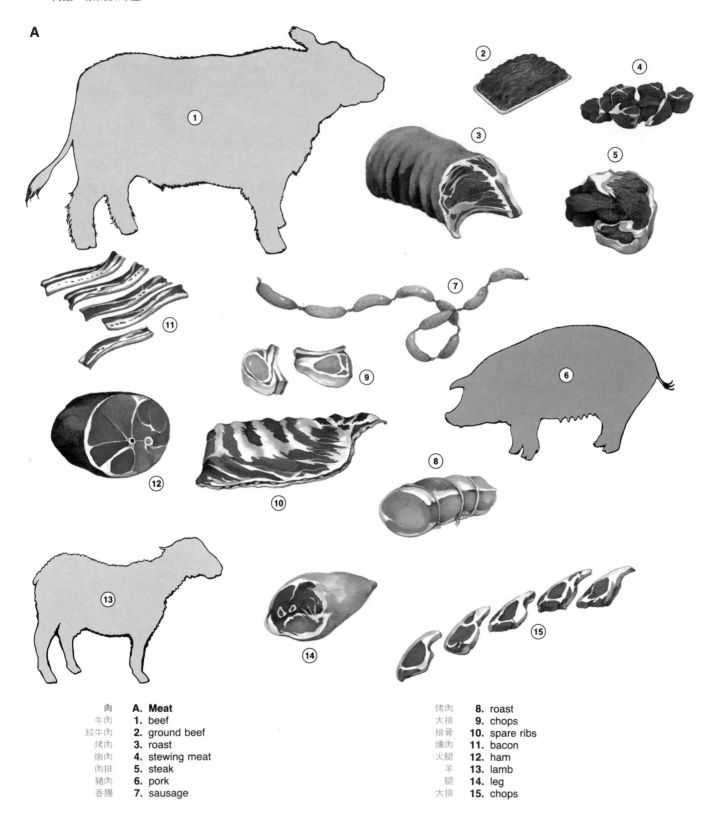

肉	**A. Meat**		烤肉	**8.** roast
牛肉	**1.** beef		大排	**9.** chops
絞牛肉	**2.** ground beef		排骨	**10.** spare ribs
烤肉	**3.** roast		燻肉	**11.** bacon
燉肉	**4.** stewing meat		火腿	**12.** ham
肉排	**5.** steak		羊	**13.** lamb
豬肉	**6.** pork		腿	**14.** leg
香腸	**7.** sausage		大排	**15.** chops

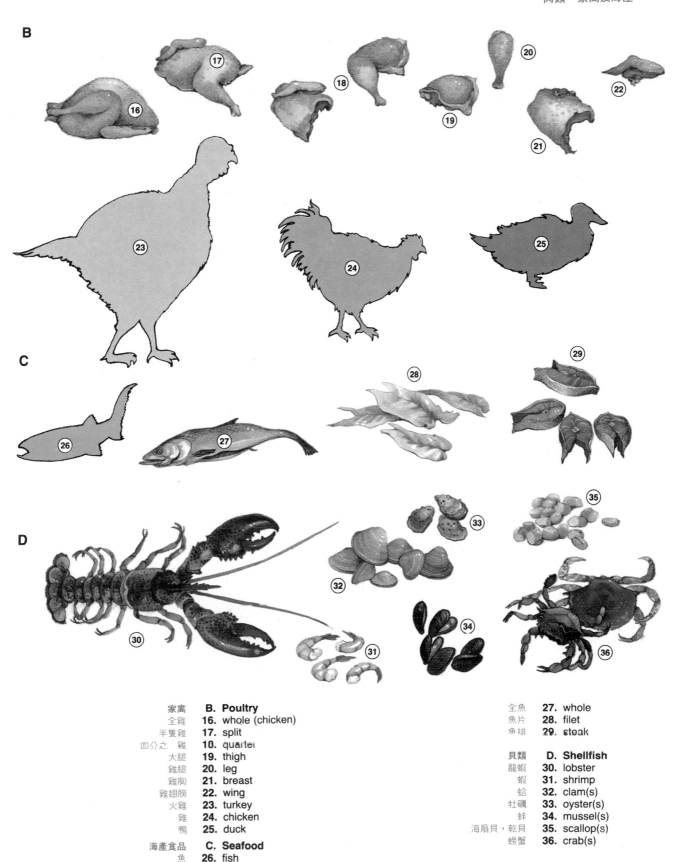

B

C

D

家禽	**B. Poultry**
全雞	**16.** whole (chicken)
半隻雞	**17.** split
四分之一雞	**18.** quarter
大腿	**19.** thigh
雞腿	**20.** leg
雞胸	**21.** breast
雞翅膀	**22.** wing
火雞	**23.** turkey
雞	**24.** chicken
鴨	**25.** duck
海產食品	**C. Seafood**
魚	**26.** fish

全魚	**27.** whole
魚片	**28.** filet
魚排	**29.** steak
貝類	**D. Shellfish**
龍蝦	**30.** lobster
蝦	**31.** shrimp
蛤	**32.** clam(s)
牡礪	**33.** oyster(s)
蚌	**34.** mussel(s)
海扇貝，乾貝	**35.** scallop(s)
螃蟹	**36.** crab(s)

條，盒	**1.**	carton
容器	**2.**	container
瓶	**3.**	bottle
包裝	**4.**	package
條，片	**5.**	stick
盒，盆	**6.**	tub

條	**7.**	loaf
袋	**8.**	bag
罐	**9.**	jar
罐	**10.**	can
卷	**11.**	roll

盒	**12.** box
半打裝	**13.** six-pack
唧筒	**14.** pump
管	**15.** tube
包	**16.** pack
本	**17.** book
根，條	**18.** bar
杯	**19.** cup
玻璃杯	**20.** glass
片	**21.** slice
塊	**22.** piece

碗	**23.** bowl
噴筒	**24.** spray can
錢	**Money**
一元鈔票	**25.** dollar bills
硬幣	**26.** coins
一分錢	**27.** penny
五分錢	**28.** nickel
一毛錢	**29.** dime
二角五分	**30.** quarter

熟食櫃臺	1. deli counter		購物籃	8. shopping basket
冷凍食品	2. frozen foods		產品	9. produce
冷凍室，冷藏器	3. freezer		走廊	10. aisle
乳酪製品	4. dairy products		烘烤食品	11. baked goods
牛奶	5. milk		麵包	12. bread
貨架	6. shelf		罐裝食品	13. canned goods
秤	7. scale		飲料	14. beverages

FISH   MEAT   POULTRY

EXPRESS LANE 10 ITEMS OR LESS

家用品	**15.** household items	出納員，收銀員	**22.** cashier
貯藏櫃	**16.** bin	輸送帶	**23.** conveyor belt
顧客	**17.** customer	雜貨	**24.** groceries
點心	**18.** snacks	袋子	**25.** bag
購物車	**19.** shopping cart	收銀櫃台	**26.** checkout counter
收據	**20.** receipt	支票	**27.** check
收銀機	**21.** cash register		

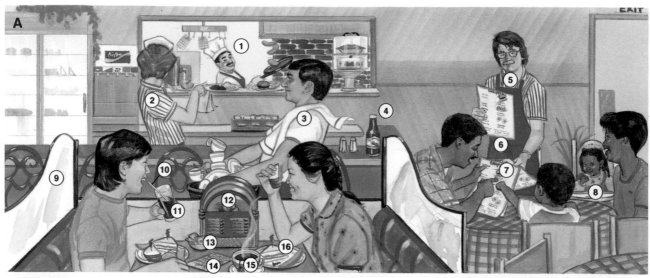

家庭餐館	A. Family Restaurant	酒吧間	B. Cocktail Lounge
廚子	1. cook	拔塞鑽	17. corkscrew
女侍者	2. waitress	塞子	18. cork
茶房	3. busboy	果酒	19. wine
蕃茄醬	4. ketchup	栓，塞	20. tap
侍者	5. waiter	酒保	21. bartender
圍裙	6. apron	酒(瓶)	22. liquor (bottle)
菜單	7. menu	啤酒	23. beer
高座椅	8. high chair	酒吧	24. bar
雅座，隔房座位	9. booth	酒吧椅	25. bar stool
吸管	10. straw	煙斗	26. pipe
軟飲料	11. soft drink	杯墊	27. coaster
自動點唱機	12. jukebox	(一包)火柴	28. (book of) matches
糖(包)	13. sugar (packet)	煙灰缸	29. ashtray
帳單	14. check	打火機	30. lighter
茶	15. tea	香煙	31. cigarette
三明治	16. sandwich	酒店女招待	32. cocktail waitress
		托盤	33. tray

吃	**1.** eat	擺(飯桌)	**8.** set (the table)
喝	**2.** drink	給	**9.** give
服侍	**3.** serve	拿	**10.** take
作飯	**4.** cook	抹	**11.** spread
點菜	**5.** order	拿	**12.** hold
收拾	**6.** clear	點燃	**13.** light
付錢	**7.** pay	燙	**14.** burn

茶茉	1. mustard
熱狗	2. hot dog
燉豆	3. baked beans
蕃薯片	4. potato chips
薄餅	5. pancakes
糖漿	6. syrup
麵包捲	7. bun
醃黃瓜	8. pickle
漢堡	9. hamburger
通心粉	10. spaghetti
肉丸	11. meatballs
沙拉汁	12. salad dressing
沙拉	13. tossed salad
燉牛肉	14. beef stew
豬排	15. pork chops
各色蔬菜	16. mixed vegetables
芋泥	17. mashed potatoes
牛油	18. butter

麵包捲	19. roll
烤馬鈴薯	20. baked potato
牛排	21. steak
餅乾	22. cookie
聖代	23. sundae
塔哥	24. taco
春捲	25. egg roll
草莓餅	26. strawberry shortcake
烤麵糰	27. biscuit
炸馬鈴薯條	28. french fries
炸雞	29. fried chicken
義大利脆餅	30. pizza
水果凍	31. jelly
(單面煎)荷包蛋	32. (sunnyside-up) egg
燻肉	33. bacon
吐司麵包	34. toast
咖啡	35. coffee
冰淇淋捲	36. ice cream cone

手套	**1.** gloves	緊身衣	**14.** tights
帽子	**2.** cap	冰	**15.** ice skates
法蘭絨襯衫	**3.** flannel shirt	滑雪帽	**16.** ski cap
背袋	**4.** backpack	茄克	**17.** jacket
防風衣	**5.** windbreaker	帽子	**18.** hat
牛仔褲	**6.** (blue) jeans	圍巾	**19.** scarf
(圓領)毛衣	**7.** (crewneck) sweater	長大衣	**20.** overcoat
半長羽絨衣	**8.** parka	靴子	**21.** boots
遠足靴	**9.** hiking boots	貝雷帽	**22.** beret
禦寒耳罩	**10.** earmuffs	(雞心領)毛衣	**23.** (V-neck) sweater
手套	**11.** mittens	外套	**24.** coat
羽絨背心	**12.** down vest	雨靴	**25.** rain boots
(高領)毛衣	**13.** (turtleneck) sweater		

衣領	**1.** lapel		短褲	**14.** shorts
運動上裝	**2.** blazer		長袖	**15.** long sleeve
鈕扣	**3.** button		皮帶	**16.** belt
便褲，家常褲	**4.** slacks		皮帶扣	**17.** buckle
鞋跟	**5.** heel		購物袋	**18.** shopping bag
鞋底	**6.** sole		涼鞋	**19.** sandal
鞋帶	**7.** shoelace		領子	**20.** collar
運動長袖衫	**8.** sweatshirt		短袖	**21.** short sleeve
皮夾	**9.** wallet		洋裝	**22.** dress
運動長褲	**10.** sweatpants		皮包	**23.** purse
軟底鞋	**11.** sneakers		雨傘	**24.** umbrella
汗巾帶	**12.** sweatband		高跟鞋	**25.** (high) heels
背心	**13.** tank top			

羊毛上衣	**26.** cardigan
（燈心絨）長褲	**27.** (corduroy) pants
硬帽	**28.** hard hat
T恤衫	**29.** T-shirt
工作服	**30.** overalls
午餐盒	**31.** lunch box
（工作）靴	**32.** (construction) boots
外套	**33.** jacket
女襯衫	**34.** blouse
（有肩帶的）女用手提包	**35.** (shoulder) bag
裙子	**36.** skirt
公事包	**37.** briefcase

風衣	**38.** raincoat
背心	**39.** vest
三件式西服	**40.** three-piece suit
口袋	**41.** pocket
便鞋	**42.** loafer
制帽	**43.** cap
眼鏡	**44.** glasses
制服	**45.** uniform
襯衫	**46.** shirt
領帶	**47.** tie
報紙	**48.** newspaper
皮鞋	**49.** shoe

內衣	**1.** undershirt	女用貼身短內褲	**12.** briefs
男用短內褲	**2.** boxer shorts	胸罩	**13.** bra(ssiere)
內褲	**3.** underpants	襪帶	**14.** garter belt
護襠褲	**4.** athletic supporter	束腰衣	**15.** girdle
褲襪	**5.** pantyhose	及膝長襪	**16.** knee socks
絲襪	**6.** stockings	短襪	**17.** socks
綿毛衫褲	**7.** long johns	拖鞋	**18.** slippers
襯裙	**8.** half slip	睡衣	**19.** pajamas
女用緊身衣	**9.** camisole	浴泡	**20.** bathrobe
連身襯裙	**10.** full slip	睡衣	**21.** nightgown
比基尼式三角褲	**11.** (bikini) panties		

珠寶	**A. Jewelry**		梳洗化粧用品	**B. Toiletries and Makeup**
耳環	1. earrings		刮鬍刀	20. razor
戒指	2. ring(s)		刮鬍後用的面霜	21. after-shave lotion
訂婚戒指	3. engagement ring		刮鬍膏	22. shaving cream
結婚戒指	4. wedding ring		剃刀	23. razor blades
鍊子	5. chain		指甲銼	24. emery board
項鍊	6. necklace		指甲油	25. nail polish
珠鍊	7. (strand of) beads		眉筆	26. eyebrow pencil
胸針	8. pin		香水	27. perfume
手環	9. bracelet		畫睫筆	28. mascara
手錶	10. watch		口紅	29. lipstick
錶帶	11. watchband		眼影	30. eye shadow
袖扣	12. cuff links		指甲刀	31. nail clippers
領帶扣	13. tie pin		刷子	32. blush
領帶夾	14. tie clip		眼線筆	33. eyeliner
扣耳環	15. clip-on earring			
穿洞耳環	16. pierced earring			
扣鍊	17. clasp			
耳穿	18. post			
背扣	19. back			

短	**1.** short	
長	**2.** long	
緊	**3.** tight	
鬆	**4.** loose	
髒	**5.** dirty	
乾淨	**6.** clean	
小	**7.** small	
大	**8.** big	
淺	**9.** light	
深	**10.** dark	
高	**11.** high	

低	**12.** low
新	**13.** new
舊	**14.** old
開着	**15.** open
關着	**16.** closed
條紋	**17.** striped
方格	**18.** checked
圓點	**19.** polka dot
單色	**20.** solid
印花	**21.** print
格子	**22.** plaid

下雨	**1.** rainy		涼爽	**9.** cool
多雲	**2.** cloudy		寒冷	**10.** cold
下雪	**3.** snowy		冰點	**11.** freezing
晴	**4.** sunny		多霧	**12.** foggy
溫度計	**5.** thermometer		刮風	**13.** windy
溫度	**6.** temperature		乾燥	**14.** dry
熱	**7.** hot		潮濕	**15.** wet
暖和	**8.** warm		冰滴	**16.** icy

春天	**Spring**	夏天	**Summer**	秋天	**Fall**	冬天	**Winter**
油漆	**1.** paint	澆水	**5.** water	裝	**9.** fill	剷雪	**13.** shovel
清洗	**2.** clean	割草,剪草	**6.** mow	刨草	**10.** rake	沙	**14.** sand
挖	**3.** dig	拔	**7.** pick	砍	**11.** chop	刮	**15.** scrape
種植	**4.** plant	修剪	**8.** trim	推	**12.** push	背	**16.** carry

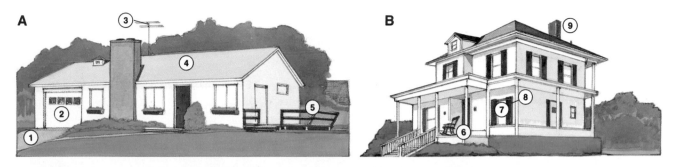

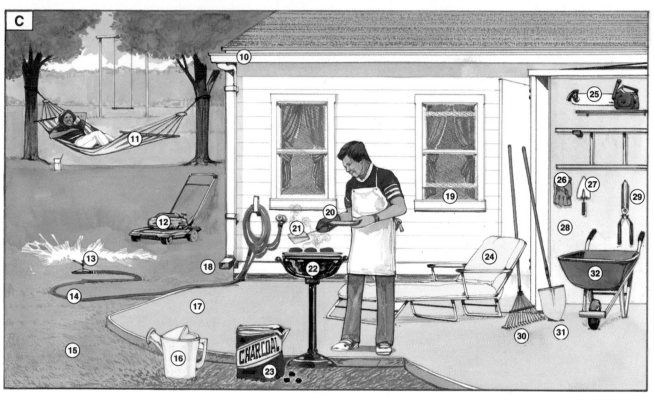

牧場式房子	**A. Ranch House**
車道	**1.** driveway
車房	**2.** garage
電視天線	**3.** TV antenna
屋頂	**4.** roof
平台	**5.** deck

殖民式房子	**B. Colonial-style House**
陽台	**6.** porch
窗戶	**7.** window
百葉窗	**8.** shutter
煙囪	**9.** chimney

後院	**C. The Backyard**
排水管	**10.** gutter
吊床	**11.** hammock
割草機	**12.** lawn mower
噴嘴	**13.** sprinkler
皮管	**14.** garden hose

草地	**15.** grass
噴水壺	**16.** watering can
天井台	**17.** patio
導水管	**18.** drainpipe
紗窗	**19.** screen
手套	**20.** mitt
小鏟	**21.** spatula
烤架	**22.** grill
煤球	**23.** charcoal briquettes
躺椅	**24.** lounge chair
電鋸	**25.** power saw
工作手套	**26.** work gloves
鏟子	**27.** trowel
工作房	**28.** toolshed
樹剪	**29.** hedge clippers
耙子	**30.** rake
鏟子，鐵鍬	**31.** shovel
獨輪車	**32.** wheelbarrow

吊扇	**1.** ceiling fan		靠背沙發	**16.** recliner
天花板	**2.** ceiling		遙控器	**17.** remote control
牆	**3.** wall		電視	**18.** television
畫框	**4.** frame		組合櫃	**19.** wall unit
畫	**5.** painting		音響系統	**20.** stereo system
花瓶	**6.** vase		擴聲機	**21.** speaker
壁台	**7.** mantel		書架	**22.** bookcase
壁爐	**8.** fireplace		窗簾	**23.** drapes
火	**9.** fire		椅墊	**24.** cushion
圓形木材	**10.** log		沙發	**25.** sofa
樓梯扶手	**11.** banister		茶几	**26.** coffee table
樓梯	**12.** staircase		燈罩	**27.** lampshade
梯階	**13.** step		燈	**28.** lamp
書桌	**14.** desk		邊桌	**29.** end table
地毯	**15.** wall-to-wall carpeting			

瓷器	**1.** china		桌布	**16.** tablecloth
瓷器櫃	**2.** china closet		椅子	**17.** chair
吊燈	**3.** chandelier		咖啡壺	**18.** coffeepot
水壺	**4.** pitcher		茶壺	**19.** teapot
酒杯	**5.** wine glass		茶杯，杯子	**20.** cup
水杯	**6.** water glass		碟子	**21.** saucer
桌子	**7.** table		銀器	**22.** silverware
湯匙	**8.** spoon		糖碗	**23.** sugar bowl
胡椒瓶	**9.** pepper shaker		奶油瓶	**24.** creamer
鹽瓶	**10.** salt shaker		沙拉碗	**25.** salad bowl
牛油麵包托盤	**11.** bread and butter plate		火焰	**26.** flame
叉子	**12.** fork		燃燭	**27.** candle
盤子	**13.** plate		燭臺	**28.** candlestick
餐巾	**14.** napkin		餐具櫥	**29.** buffet
刀子	**15.** knife			

洗碗機	**1.** dishwasher		擦碗布	**18.** dish towel
碗盤架	**2.** dish drainer		冰箱	**19.** refrigerator
蒸架	**3.** steamer		冷凍櫃	**20.** freezer
開罐器	**4.** can opener		冰盒	**21.** ice tray
平底鍋	**5.** frying pan		碗櫥	**22.** cabinet
開瓶器	**6.** bottle opener		微波爐烤箱	**23.** microwave oven
濾器	**7.** colander		攪拌皿	**24.** mixing bowl
燉鍋	**8.** saucepan		桿麵杖	**25.** rolling pin
蓋子	**9.** lid		切菜板	**26.** cutting board
洗潔精	**10.** dishwashing liquid		廚桌臺	**27.** counter
擦墊	**11.** scouring pad		茶壺	**28.** teakettle
攪和器	**12.** blender		煤氣爐	**29.** burner
鍋子	**13.** pot		爐臺	**30.** stove
瓦瓷鍋	**14.** casserole dish		煮咖啡器	**31.** coffeemaker
罐子	**15.** canister		烤箱	**32.** oven
烤麵包機	**16.** toaster		焙箱	**33.** broiler
烤盤	**17.** roasting pan		隔熱墊	**34.** pot holder

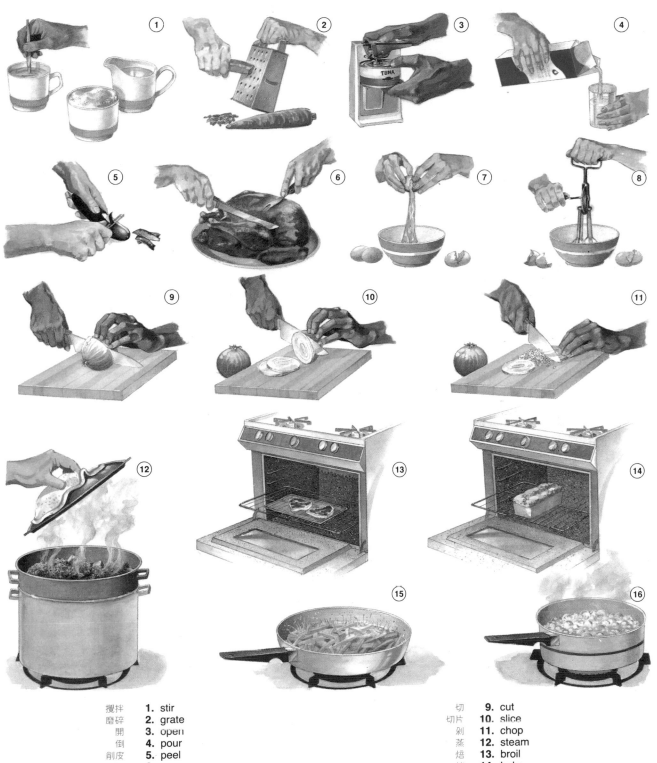

攪拌	**1.** stir	切	**9.** cut
磨碎	**2.** grate	切片	**10.** slice
開	**3.** open	剁	**11.** chop
倒	**4.** pour	蒸	**12.** steam
削皮	**5.** peel	焙	**13.** broil
切	**6.** carve	烤	**14.** bake
打，敲	**7.** break	炸	**15.** fry
打	**8.** beat	煮	**16.** boil

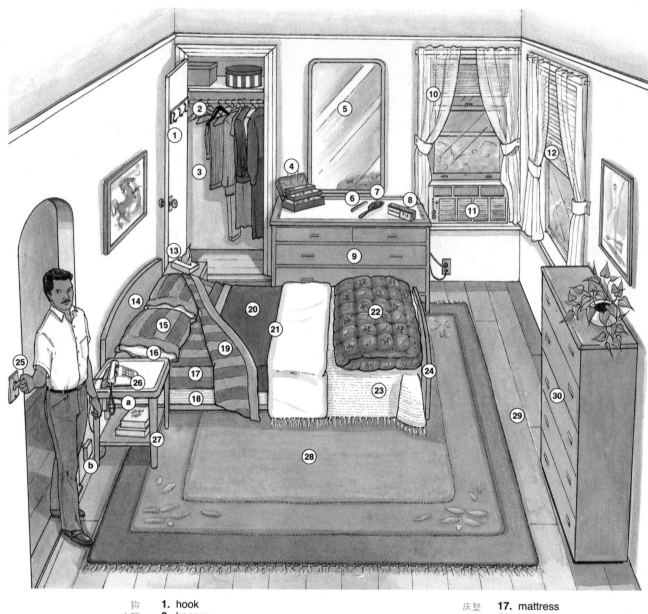

鉤	**1.** hook	床墊	**17.** mattress
衣架	**2.** hanger	彈簧	**18.** box spring
櫃子	**3.** closet	床單	**19.** (flat) sheet
珠寶盒	**4.** jewelry box	毯子	**20.** blanket
鏡子	**5.** mirror	床	**21.** bed
梳子	**6.** comb	被子	**22.** comforter
頭刷	**7.** hairbrush	床罩	**23.** bedspread
鬧鐘	**8.** alarm clock	床腳架	**24.** footboard
抽屜	**9.** bureau	開關	**25.** light switch
窗帘	**10.** curtain	電話	**26.** phone
空調器，冷氣機	**11.** air conditioner	電話線	**a.** cord
百葉窗	**12.** blinds	線盒	**b.** jack
面紙	**13.** tissues	床頭桌	**27.** night table
床頭板	**14.** headboard	地毯	**28.** rug
枕頭套	**15.** pillowcase	地板	**29.** floor
枕頭	**16.** pillow	五斗櫃	**30.** chest of drawers

捲簾	**1.** shade		奶嘴	**18.** nipple
活動懸掛玩具	**2.** mobile		鬆緊嬰兒衣	**19.** stretchie
玩具熊	**3.** teddy bear		圍兜	**20.** bib
嬰兒床，有欄臥牀	**4.** crib		響鈴	**21.** rattle
嬰兒床側墊	**5.** bumper		奶嘴	**22.** pacifier
嬰兒乳液	**6.** baby lotion		學步車	**23.** walker
痱子粉	**7.** baby power		鞦韆	**24.** swing
嬰兒擦	**8.** baby wipes		玩具房屋	**25.** doll house
嬰兒桌	**9.** changing table		搖籃	**26.** cradle
棉花棒	**10.** cotton swab		充塞動物玩具	**27.** stuffed animal
安全別針	**11.** safety pin		洋娃娃	**28.** doll
（用後即棄的）尿布	**12.** disposable diaper		玩具箱	**29.** toy chest
布製尿布	**13.** cloth diaper		嬰兒圍欄	**30.** playpen
嬰兒推車	**14.** stroller		拼謎	**31.** puzzle
火警器	**15.** smoke detector		拼塊	**32.** block
搖椅	**16.** rocking chair		嬰兒用馬桶	**33.** potty
奶瓶	**17.** bottle			

帘架	1. curtain rod	熱水龍頭	17. hot water faucet
帘環	2. curtain rings	冷水龍頭	18. cold water faucet
浴帽	3. shower cap	水槽	19. sink
蓮蓬頭	4. shower head	指甲刷	20. nailbrush
浴帘	5. shower curtain	牙刷	21. toothbrush
肥皂缸	6. soap dish	抹布	22. washcloth
海綿	7. sponge	手巾	23. hand towel
洗髮精	8. shampoo	浴巾	24. bath towel
出水口	9. drain	毛巾架	25. towel rack
水塞	10. stopper	吹風機	26. hair dryer
浴缸	11. bathtub	瓷磚	27. tile
浴墊	12. bath mat	髒衣簍	28. hamper
垃圾桶	13. wastepaper basket	馬桶	29. toilet
醫藥櫃	14. medicine chest	衛生紙	30. toilet paper
肥皂	15. soap	馬桶刷	31. toilet brush
牙膏	16. toothpaste	秤	32. scale

人字梯	**1.** stepladder		配件	**17.** attachments
雞毛撣子	**2.** feather duster		管子	**18.** pipe
手電筒	**3.** flashlight		晾衣繩	**19.** clothesline
碎布	**4.** rags		衣夾	**20.** clothespins
電閘刀	**5.** circuit breaker		漿衣劑	**21.** spray starch
(海綿)拖把	**6.** (sponge) mop		燈泡	**22.** lightbulb
掃帚	**7.** broom		紙巾	**23.** paper towels
簸箕	**8.** dustpan		烘乾機	**24.** dryer
清潔劑	**9.** cleanser		洗衣粉	**25.** laundry detergent
擦窗劑	**10.** window cleaner		漂白劑	**26.** bleach
拖把更換頭	**11.** (mop) refill		纖維柔軟劑	**27.** fabric softener
熨斗	**12.** iron		洗滌物	**28.** laundry
熨衣板	**13.** ironing board		洗衣籃	**29.** laundry basket
通廁器	**14.** plunger		洗衣機	**30.** washing machine
桶子	**15.** bucket		垃圾桶	**31.** garbage can
吸塵器	**16.** vacuum cleaner		抓鼠器	**32.** mousetrap

木工尺	**1.** carpenter's rule		鐵槌	**13.** hammer
咬合鉗	**2.** C-clamp		刮刀	**14.** scraper
電動手鋸	**3.** jigsaw		掛鈎板	**15.** pegboard
木頭，木板	**4.** wood		掛鈎	**16.** hook
電線延長線	**5.** extension cord		手斧	**17.** hatchet
電插座	**6.** outlet		鋼鋸	**18.** hacksaw
接地插頭	**7.** grounding plug		鉗子	**19.** pliers
鋸子	**8.** saw		圓形鋸	**20.** circular saw
曲柄鑽子	**9.** brace		捲尺	**21.** tape measure
螺旋鉗	**10.** wrench		工作台	**22.** workbench
木槌	**11.** mallet		工具箱	**23.** toolbox
活扳手	**12.** monkey wrench			

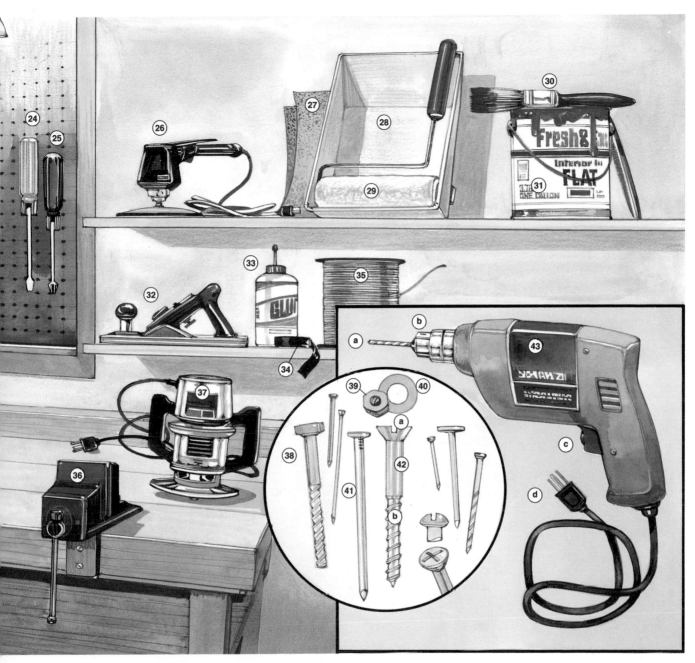

螺絲起子	**24.** screwdriver	打線機	**37.** router
多角螺絲起子	**25.** Phillips screwdriver	螺釘	**38.** bolt
電動磨光機	**26.** power sander	螺帽	**39.** nut
沙紙	**27.** sandpaper	皮圈	**40.** washer
盤	**28.** pan	釘子	**41.** nail
滾筒	**29.** roller	螺絲釘	**42.** screw
油漆刷	**30.** paintbrush	釘頭	**a.** head
油漆	**31.** paint	螺紋	**b.** thread
刨刀	**32.** wood plane	電鑽	**43.** electric drill
膠水	**33.** glue	鑽頭	**a.** bit
絕緣膠布	**34.** electrical tape	軸	**b.** shank
電線	**35.** wire	開關	**c.** switch
虎頭鉗	**36.** vise	插頭	**d.** plug

家事及修理用詞(動詞)

疊	**1.** fold
刷	**2.** scrub
擦亮	**3.** polish
轉緊	**4.** tighten
擦，抹	**5.** wipe
掛	**6.** hang
掃	**7.** sweep
鋪(床)	**8.** make (the bed)

擦乾	**9.** dry
修理	**10.** repair
熨	**11.** iron
上油	**12.** oil
換(床單)	**13.** change (the sheets)
吸塵	**14.** vacuum
撢灰	**15.** dust
洗	**16.** wash

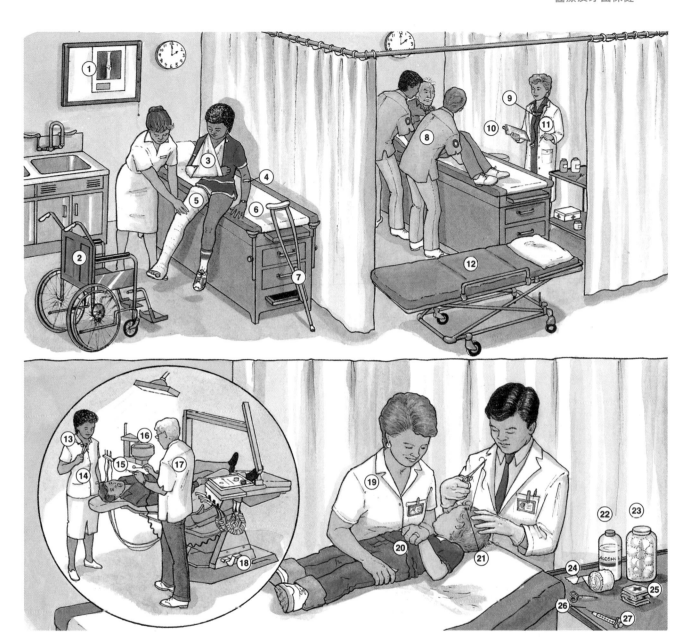

X光	**1.** X-ray	牙鑽	**15.** drill
輪椅	**2.** wheelchair	水盆	**16.** basin
三角巾	**3.** sling	牙醫	**17.** dentist
膠布	**4.** Band-Aid	踏板	**18.** pedal
石膏	**5.** cast	護士	**19.** nurse
檢查床	**6.** examining table	病人	**20.** patient
拐杖	**7.** crutch	縫針	**21.** stitches
服務員	**8.** attendant	酒精	**22.** alcohol
聽診器	**9.** stethoscope	棉花球	**23.** cotton balls
病歷表	**10.** chart	(紗布)繃帶	**24.** (gauze) bandage
醫生	**11.** doctor	紗布墊	**25.** gauze pads
擔架	**12.** stretcher	針	**26.** needle
儀器	**13.** instruments	注射器	**27.** syringe
口腔保健師	**14.** oral hygienist		

紅腫	**1.** rash
發燒	**2.** fever
蟲咬傷	**3.** insect bite
發冷	**4.** chills
黑眼圈	**5.** black eye
頭疼	**6.** headache
胃疼	**7.** stomachache
背疼	**8.** backache
牙疼	**9.** toothache
高血壓	**10.** high blood pressure

感冒	**11.** cold
喉嚨疼	**12.** sore throat
壓舌板	**a.** tongue depressor
扭傷	**13.** sprain
繃帶	**a.** stretch bandage
感染	**14.** infection
骨折	**15.** broken bone
切傷	**16.** cut
青腫	**17.** bruise
燙傷	**18.** burn

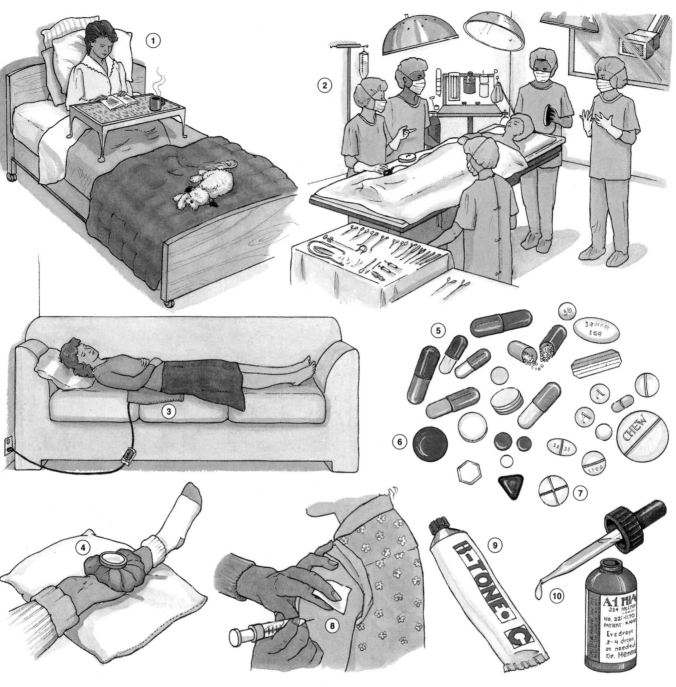

臥床休息	**1.** bed rest	藥品	**Medicine**
外科手術	**2.** surgery	膠囊	**5.** capsule
加熱墊	**3.** heating pad	藥片	**6.** tablet
冰袋	**4.** ice pack	藥丸	**7.** pill
		注射	**8.** injection
		藥膏	**9.** ointment
		眼藥水	**10.** eye drops

梯子	**1.** ladder		消防隊員	**10.** fire fighter
消防車	**2.** fire engine		減火器	**11.** fire extinguisher
消防車	**3.** fire truck		消防盔	**12.** helmet
防火梯	**4.** fire escape		消防外套	**13.** coat
火	**5.** fire		斧頭	**14.** ax
救護車	**6.** ambulance		煙	**15.** smoke
救護人員	**7.** paramedic		水	**16.** water
水管	**8.** hose		噴嘴	**17.** nozzle
消防龍頭	**9.** fire hydrant			

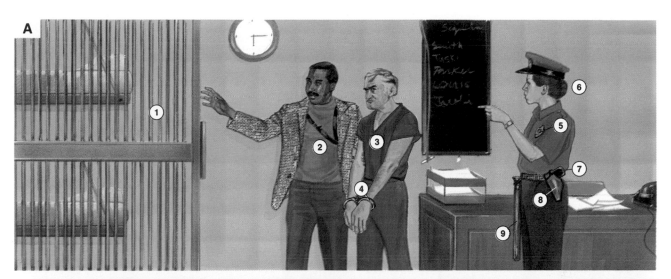

警察局	**A. Police Station**		槌	**12.** gavel
監牢	**1.** jail		證人	**13.** witness
偵探	**2.** detective		法庭紀錄人	**14.** court reporter
疑犯	**3.** suspect		法庭紀錄	**15.** transcript
手銬	**4.** handcuffs		法官席	**16.** bench
名牌	**5.** badge		檢方律師	**17.** prosecuting attorney
警官	**6.** police officer		證人席	**18.** witness stand
槍	**7.** gun		法警	**19.** court officer
槍套	**8.** holster		陪審席	**20.** jury box
警棍	**9.** nightstick		陪審團	**21.** jury
			辯護律師	**22.** defense attorney
法庭	**B. Court**		被告	**23.** defendant
法官	**10.** judge		指紋	**24.** fingerprints
法官服	**11.** robes			

辦公大樓	**1.** office building		郵局	**9.** post office
大廳	**2.** lobby		交通警察	**10.** traffic cop
角落	**3.** corner		交叉口	**11.** intersection
行人穿越道	**4.** crosswalk		行人	**12.** pedestrian
百貨公司	**5.** department store		公共汽車站	**13.** bus stop
糕餅店	**6.** bakery		長椅	**14.** bench
公共電話	**7.** public telephone		垃圾簍	**15.** trash basket
路標	**8.** street sign		地下車站	**16.** subway station

電梯	**17.** elevator	人行道	**25.** sidewalk
書店	**18.** bookstore	人行道邊沿	**26.** curb
車庫	**19.** parking garage	嬰兒車	**27.** baby carriage
停車儀表	**20.** parking motor	蔬菜水果店	**28.** fruit and vegetable market
交通燈	**21.** traffic light	街燈	**29.** streetlight
藥房	**22.** drugstore	報攤	**30.** newsstand
公寓	**23.** apartment house	街道	**31.** street
樓號	**24.** building number	下水道檢查口	**32.** manhole

遞送郵件	**A. Delivering Mail**		郵局	**B. The Post Office**
信箱	**1.** mailbox		投件口	**13.** mail slot
郵件	**2.** mail		郵政人員	**14.** postal worker
郵差	**3.** letter carrier		窗口	**15.** window
郵袋	**4.** mailbag			
郵車	**5.** mail truck		郵件種類	**C. Types of Mail**
郵筒	**6.** U.S. mailbox		(航空)信封	**16.** (airmail) envelope
信	**7.** letter		明信片	**17.** postcard
回函地址	**8.** return address		匯票	**18.** money order
郵戳	**9.** postmark		包裹	**19.** package
郵票	**10.** stamp		繩子	**20.** string
地址	**11.** address		標貼	**21.** label
郵遞區號	**12.** zip code		膠帶	**22.** tape
			快遞	**23.** Express Mail (package)

The labels in the illustration read: SUBJECT; 332-346, 347-369; 370-422, 423-574; 575-613, 614-623; 624-702, 703-746; 972 Bridenbaugh, Carl, Early Americans, 294p 1981 History-US; AMERICAN JOURNAL 1940-1950; TIME; INFORMATION; A B C D E F G H I J K L M N O P Q R S T U V W X Y Z

圖書館辦事員	1. library clerk
借書臺	2. checkout desk
圖書證	3. library card
目錄	4. card catalog
抽屜	5. drawer
書卡	6. call card
書號	7. call number
作者	8. author
書名	9. title
主題	10. subject
列，排	11. row
書名便條	12. call slip
縮影膠片	13. microfilm

縮影閱讀器	14. microfilm reader
期刊部	15. periodicals section
雜誌	16. magazine
陳列室	17. rack
影印機	18. photocopy machine
地球儀	19. globe
地圖	20. atlas
參考部	21. reference section
詢問處	22. information desk
(參考)圖書館員	23. (reference) librarian
字典	24. dictionary
百科全書	25. encyclopedia
書架	26. shelf

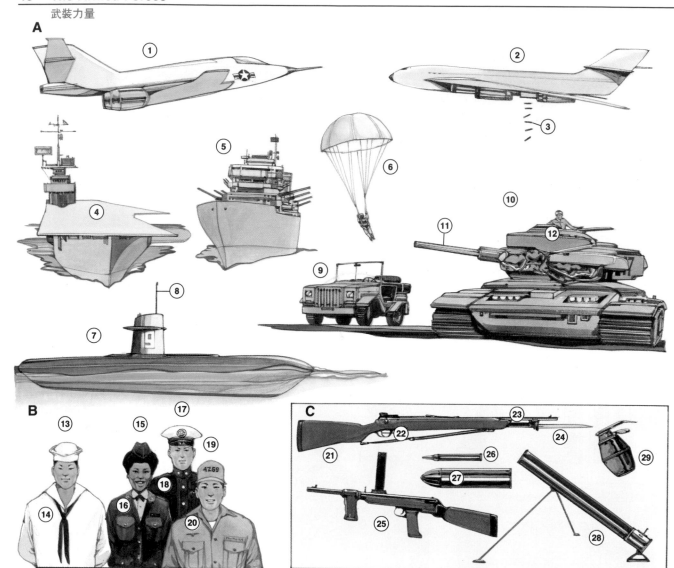

車輛及裝備	**A. Vehicles and Equipment**
戰鬪機	**1.** fighter plane
轟炸機	**2.** bomber
炸彈	**3.** bomb
航空母艦	**4.** aircraft carrier
戰艦	**5.** battleship
降落傘	**6.** parachute
潛水艇	**7.** submarine
潛望鏡	**8.** periscope
吉普車	**9.** jeep
坦克車	**10.** tank
砲	**11.** cannon
砲塔	**12.** gun turret

人員	**B. Personnel**
海軍	**13.** Navy
水手	**14.** sailor

陸軍	**15.** Army
士兵	**16.** soldier
海軍陸戰隊	**17.** Marines
海軍	**18.** marine
空軍	**19.** Air Force
飛行員	**20.** airman

武器及彈藥	**C. Weapons and Ammunition**
步槍	**21.** rifle
板機	**22.** trigger
槍	**23.** barrel
刺刀	**24.** bayonet
機關槍	**25.** machine gun
子彈	**26.** bullet
彈殼，砲彈	**27.** shell
迫擊砲	**28.** mortar
手榴彈	**29.** hand grenade

掃路車	**1.** street cleaner	送貨員	**10.** delivery person
拖車	**2.** tow truck	搬運卡車	**11.** moving van
油罐車	**3.** fuel truck	搬運員	**12.** mover
小貨車	**4.** pickup truck	水泥車	**13.** cement truck
剷雪車	**5.** snow plow	自卸車	**14.** dump truck
垃圾車	**6.** garbage truck	拖曳機	**15.** tractor trailer
清潔工	**7.** sanitation worker	卡車司機	**16.** truck driver
流動餐車	**8.** lunch truck	運輸機	**17.** transporter
運貨車	**9.** panel truck	平板車	**18.** flatbed

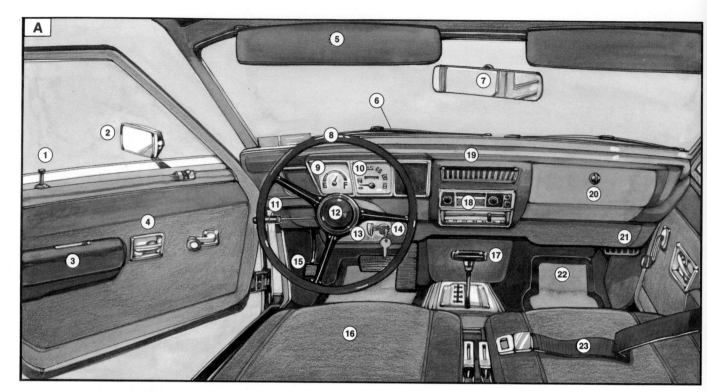

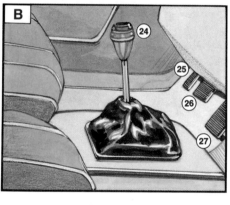

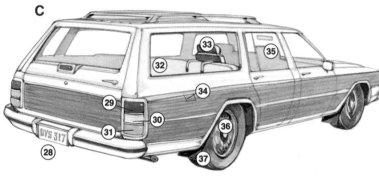

自動排檔	**A. Automatic Transmission**		排氣孔	**21.** vent
門鎖	**1.** door lock		脚垫	**22.** mat
側鏡	**2.** side mirror		安全帶	**23.** seat belt
扶手	**3.** armrest			
門把	**4.** door handle		手排檔	**B. Manual Transmission**
遮陽板	**5.** visor		排檔	**24.** stick shift
雨擦	**6.** windshield wiper		離合器	**25.** clutch
後視鏡	**7.** rearview mirror		煞車	**26.** brake
方向盤	**8.** steering wheel		油門	**27.** accelerator
油量表	**9.** gas gauge			
車速表	**10.** speedometer		旅行車	**C. Station Wagon**
方向燈操作桿	**11.** turn signal lever		牌照	**28.** license plate
喇叭	**12.** horn		煞車燈	**29.** brake light
圓柱	**13.** column		倒車燈	**30.** back-up light
發火裝置	**14.** ignition		尾燈	**31.** taillight
緊急煞車	**15.** emergency brake		後座	**32.** backseat
單人圓背摺椅	**16.** bucket seat		兒童車座	**33.** child's seat
變速器	**17.** gearshift		油箱	**34.** gas tank
收音機	**18.** radio		頭枕	**35.** headrest
儀器板	**19.** dashboard		輪蓋	**36.** hubcap
手套	**20.** glove compartment		輪胎	**37.** tire

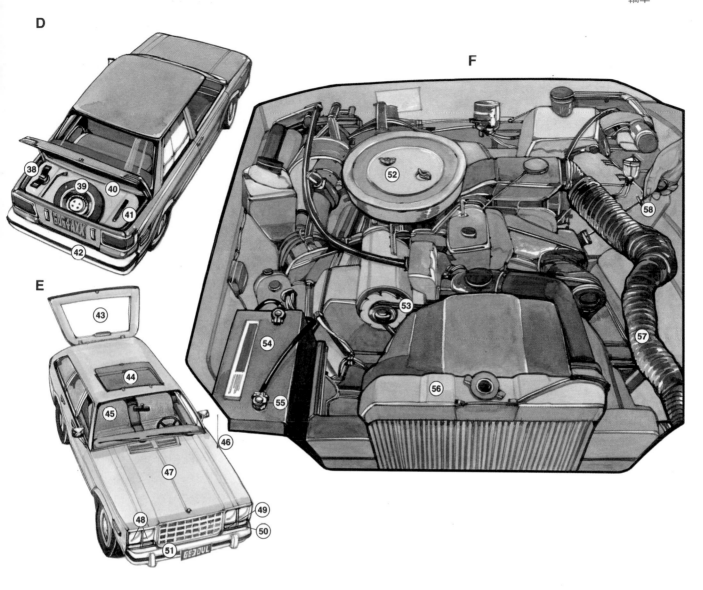

D

E

F

(雙門)轎車　　**D. (Two-door) Sedan**
千斤頂　　**38.** jack
備用胎　　**39.** spare tire
行李箱　　**40.** trunk
反光板　　**41.** flare
後緩衝擋　　**42.** rear bumper

四門後啓轎車　　**E. Four-door Hatchback**
後啓門　　**43.** hatchback
天窗　　**44.** sunroof
擋風玻璃　　**45.** windshield
天線　　**46.** antenna
車蓋　　**47.** hood

車前燈　　**48.** headlights
停車指示燈　　**49.** parking lights
轉彎信號燈　　**50.** turn signal (lights)
前緩衝擋　　**51.** front bumper

引擎　　**F. Engine**
空氣濾器　　**52.** air filter
電扇傳動帶　　**53.** fan belt
電池　　**54.** battery
電池接頭　　**55.** terminal
散熱器　　**56.** radiator
風管　　**57.** hose
機油量桿　　**58.** dipstick

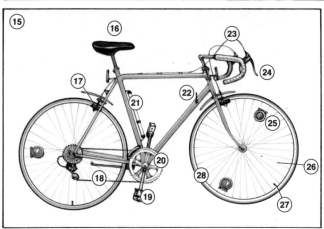

輔助輪	**1.** training wheels	傳動鏈	**18.** chain
(賽車)手把	**2.** (racing) handlebars	踏板	**19.** pedal
女式車架	**3.** girl's frame	扣鏈齒輪	**20.** sprocket
車輪	**4.** wheel	打氣筒	**21.** pump
喇叭	**5.** horn	變速器	**22.** gear changer
三輪自行車	**6.** tricycle	煞車纜	**23.** cable
頭盔	**7.** helmet	手煞車	**24.** hand brake
寬輪車	**8.** dirt bike	反光盤	**25.** reflector
撐腳架	**9.** kickstand	車輪鋼絲	**26.** spoke
擋泥板	**10.** fender	氣嘴	**27.** valve
男式車架	**11.** boy's frame	胎	**28.** tire
平車扶手	**12.** touring handlebars	機器腳踏車	**29.** motor scooter
鎖	**13.** lock	摩托車	**30.** motorcycle
自行車架	**14.** bike stand	減震器	**31.** shock absorbers
自行車	**15.** bicycle	引擎	**32.** engine
車座	**16.** seat	排氣管	**33.** exhaust pipe
煞車	**17.** brake		

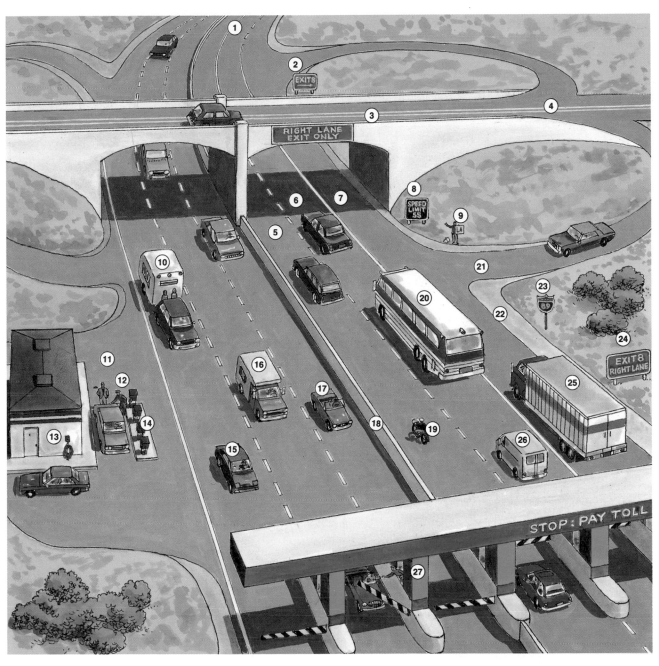

州際高速公路	**1.** interstate highway		客車	**15.** passenger car
出口道	**2.** exit ramp		露營車	**16.** camper
天橋	**3.** overpass		跑車	**17.** sports car
立體道路交叉點	**4.** cloverleaf		分向胸牆	**18.** center divider
左車道	**5.** left lane		摩托車	**19.** motorcycle
中間車道	**6.** center lane		公共汽車	**20.** bus
右車道	**7.** right lane		入口車道	**21.** entrance ramp
速限標幟	**8.** speed limit sign		路肩	**22.** shoulder
搭便車的人	**9.** hitchhiker		路標	**23.** road sign
拖曳房屋車	**10.** trailer		出口標幟	**24.** exit sign
服務區	**11.** service area		卡車	**25.** truck
服務員	**12.** attendant		大貨車，有蓋搬運車	**26.** van
氣泵	**13.** air pump		公路收費站	**27.** tollbooth
油泵	**14.** gas pump			

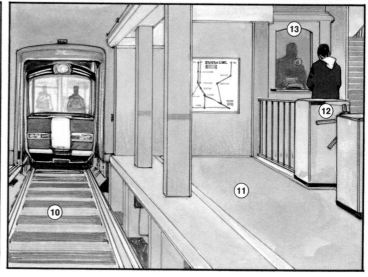

公共汽車	**A. Bus**		地下車	**B. Subway**
拉線	1. cord		列車長	7. conductor
座位	2. seat		吊環	8. strap
公車司機	3. bus driver		車廂	9. car
轉車車票	4. transfer		軌道	10. track
投幣箱	5. fare box		月臺	11. platform
乘客	6. rider		十字轉門	12. turnstile
			售票亭	13. token booth

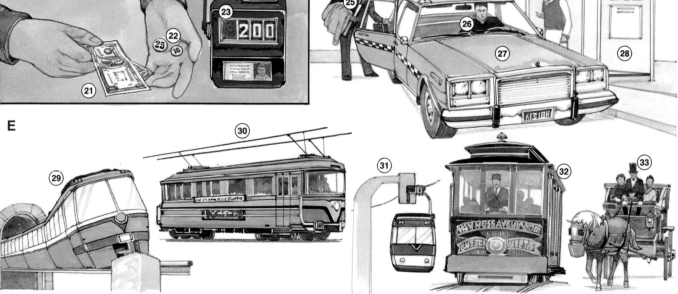

火車	**C. Train**		收據	24. receipt
通勤火車	14. commuter train		乘客	25. passenger
司機	15. engineer		計程車司機	26. cab driver
車票	16. ticket		計程車	27. taxicab
通勤者	17. commuter		計程車泊位	28. taxi stand
車站	18. station			
售票窗	19. ticket window		其他交通形式	**E. Other Forms of Transportation**
行車時刻表	20. timetable		單軌火車	29. monorail
			有軌電車	30. streetcar
計程車	**D. Taxi**		架空電車	31. aerial tramway
車費	21. fare		電纜車	32. cable car
小費	22. tip		馬車	33. horse-drawn carriage
計費表	23. meter			

機場登記	**Airport Check-In**
衣掛袋	**1.** garment bag
掛包	**2.** carry-on bag
旅客	**3.** traveler
票	**4.** ticket
搬運工	**5.** porter
輪車	**6.** dolly
衣箱	**7.** suitcase
行李	**8.** baggage

安全檢查門	**Security**
安全人員	**9.** security guard
金屬檢測器	**10.** metal detector
X光掃描器	**11.** X-ray screener
輸送帶	**12.** conveyor belt

登機	**Boarding**
駕駛艙	**13.** cockpit
儀器	**14.** instruments
駕駛員	**15.** pilot
副駕駛員	**16.** copilot
空中機械師	**17.** flight engineer
登機牌	**18.** boarding pass
機艙	**19.** cabin
機上服務員	**20.** flight attendant
行李箱	**21.** luggage compartment
折桌	**22.** tray table
走廊	**23.** aisle

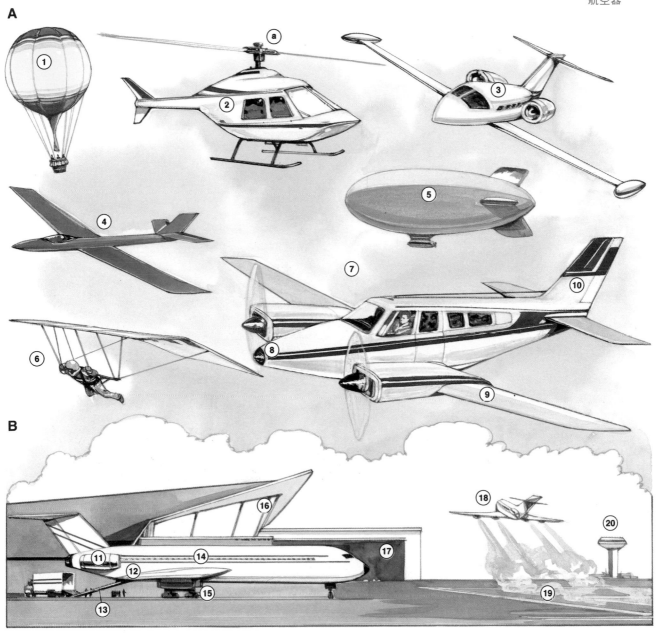

A

B

航空器類別	**A. Aircraft Types**
熱氣球	**1.** hot air balloon
直升機	**2.** helicopter
旋翼	**a.** rotor
私人噴射機	**3.** private jet
滑翔機	**4.** glider
軟式飛船	**5.** blimp
懸掛式滑翔機	**6.** hang glider
螺旋槳飛機	**7.** propeller plane
機頭	**8.** nose
機翼	**9.** wing
機尾	**10.** tail

起飛	**B. Takeoff**
噴射引擎	**11.** jet englne
貨艙	**12.** cargo area
貨艙門	**13.** cargo door
機身	**14.** fuselage
起落架	**15.** landing gear
登機樓	**16.** terminal building
機庫	**17.** hangar
(噴射)飛機	**18.** (jet) plane
跑道	**19.** runway
飛行控制塔	**20.** control tower

漁船	**1.** fishing boat	浮標	**16.** buoy
漁民	**2.** fisherman	渡輪	**17.** ferry
碼頭	**3.** pier	煙窗	**18.** smokestack
升降式電瓶車	**4.** forklift	救生艇	**19.** lifeboat
船頭	**5.** bow	跳板	**20.** gangway
起重機	**6.** crane	舷窗	**21.** porthole
貨櫃集裝箱	**7.** container	甲板	**22.** deck
船艙	**8.** hold	絞盤	**23.** windlass
貨輪	**9.** (container) ship	錨	**24.** anchor
貨物	**10.** cargo	錨鍊	**25.** line
船尾	**11.** stern	繫船柱	**26.** bollard
駁船	**12.** barge	遠洋客輪	**27.** ocean liner
拖船	**13.** tugboat	船塢	**28.** dock
燈塔	**14.** lighthouse	船站	**29.** terminal
油輪	**15.** tanker		

救生衣	**1.** life jacket		摩托艇	**13.** motorboat
獨木舟	**2.** canoe		滑水者	**14.** windsurfer
船漿	**3.** paddle		滑板	**15.** sailboard
帆船	**4.** sailboat		遊艇	**16.** cabin cruiser
舵	**5.** rudder		皮船	**17.** kayak
活動船板	**6.** centerboard		小舟	**18.** dinghy
下桁	**7.** boom		繫泊	**19.** mooring
桅	**8.** mast		吹氣筏	**20.** inflatable raft
帆	**9.** sail		槳架	**21.** oarlock
滑水者	**10.** water-skier		槳	**22.** oar
拖繩	**11.** towrope		划艇	**23.** rowboat
外懸式馬達	**12.** outboard motor			

花		**Flowers**
鬱金香	**1.**	tulip
花桿	**a.**	stem
三色紫蘿蘭	**2.**	pansy
百合花	**3.**	lily
菊花	**4.**	(chrysanthe)mum
雛菊	**5.**	daisy
金盞草	**6.**	marigold
喇叭花	**7.**	petunia
水仙花	**8.**	daffodil
水仙球莖	**a.**	bulb
番紅花	**9.**	crocus
風信子	**10.**	hyacinth
鳶尾花	**11.**	iris
蘭花	**12.**	orchid
百日草	**13.**	zinnia

梔子	**14.**	gardenia
猩猩木	**15.**	poinsettia
紫蘿蘭	**16.**	violet
毛茛，金鳳花	**17.**	buttercup
玫瑰	**18.**	rose
芽	**a.**	bud
花瓣	**b.**	petal
刺	**c.**	thorn
向日葵	**19.**	sunflower
草和穀類		**Grasses and Grains**
甘蔗	**20.**	sugarcane
稻	**21.**	rice
小麥	**22.**	wheat
燕麥	**23.**	oats
玉米	**24.**	corn

樹木	**Trees**		榆樹	**36.** elm
紅木	**25.** redwood		葉子	**a.** leaf
棕櫚	**26.** palm		冬青樹	**37.** holly
由加利樹	**27.** eucalyptus		楓樹	**38.** maple
山茱萸	**28.** dogwood			
木蘭	**29.** magnolia		其他植物	**Other Plants**
白楊	**30.** poplar		室內植物	**39.** house plants
柳	**31.** willow		仙人掌	**40.** cactus
樺樹	**32.** birch		灌木	**41.** bushes
橡樹	**33.** oak		蔓藤	**42.** vine
細枝	**a.** twig			
橡實	**b.** acorn		有毒植物	**Poisonous Plants**
松	**34.** pine		毒橡	**43.** poison oak
針	**a.** needle		野漆樹	**44.** poison sumac
松果	**b.** cone		毒藤	**45.** poison ivy
樹	**35.** tree			
樹枝	**a.** branch			
樹幹	**b.** trunk			
樹皮	**c.** bark			
樹根	**d.** root			

蝸牛	**1.** snail		蝦	**8.** shrimp
殼	**a.** shell		蟹	**9.** crab
觸角	**b.** antenna		乾貝	**10.** scallop
牡蠣	**2.** oyster		蚯蚓	**11.** worm
蚌	**3.** mussel		海蜇	**12.** jellyfish
蛞蝓	**4.** slug		觸鬚	**a.** tentacle
尤魚	**5.** squid		龍蝦	**13.** lobster
章魚	**6.** octopus		鉗	**a.** claw
海星	**7.** starfish			

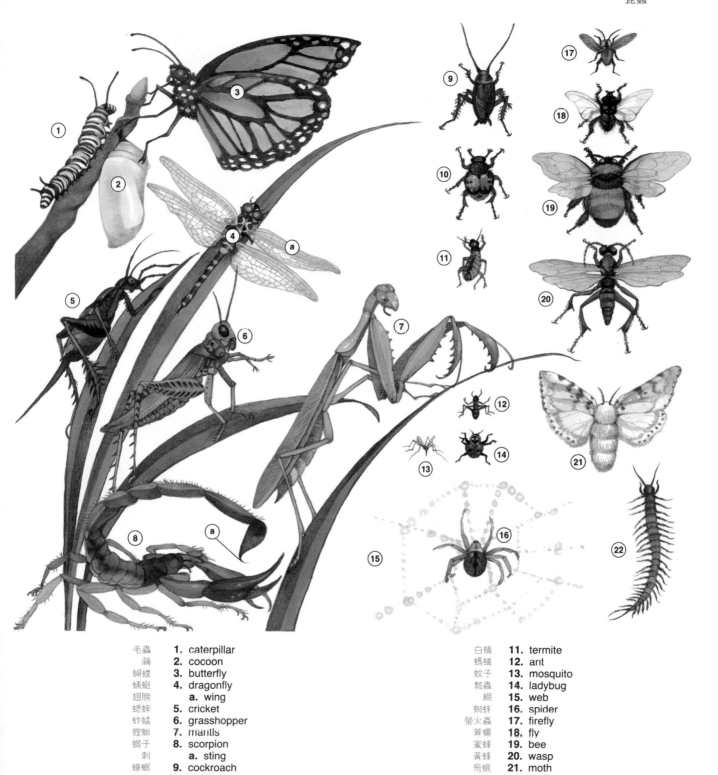

毛蟲	**1.** caterpillar		白蟻	**11.** termite
繭	**2.** cocoon		螞蟻	**12.** ant
蝴蝶	**3.** butterfly		蚊子	**13.** mosquito
蜻蜓	**4.** dragonfly		瓢蟲	**14.** ladybug
翅膀	**a.** wing		網	**15.** web
蟋蟀	**5.** cricket		蜘蛛	**16.** spider
蚱蜢	**6.** grasshopper		螢火蟲	**17.** firefly
螳螂	**7.** mantis		蒼蠅	**18.** fly
蝎子	**8.** scorpion		蜜蜂	**19.** bee
刺	**a.** sting		黃蜂	**20.** wasp
蟑螂	**9.** cockroach		飛蛾	**21.** moth
甲蟲	**10.** beetle		蜈蚣	**22.** centipede

鴿子 **1.** pigeon
翅膀 **a.** wing
蜂鳥 **2.** hummingbird
烏鴉 **3.** crow
喙 **a.** beak
海鷗 **4.** sea gull
老鷹 **5.** eagle
貓頭鷹 **6.** owl
鷹 **7.** hawk
羽毛 **a.** feather
藍樫鳥 **8.** blue jay
知更鳥 **9.** robin
麻雀 **10.** sparrow
緋鳥 **11.** cardinal
鴕鳥 **12.** ostrich
蛋 **13.** egg
金絲雀 **14.** canary
小鸚鵡 **15.** parakeet

鸚鵡 **16.** parrot
啄木鳥 **17.** woodpecker
孔雀 **18.** peacock
雉 **19.** pheasant
火雞 **20.** turkey
公雞 **21.** rooster
小雞 **22.** chick
雞 **23.** chicken
鵜鶘 **24.** pelican
嘴 **a.** bill
鴨 **25.** duck
鵝 **26.** goose
企鵝 **27.** penguin
天鵝 **28.** swan
紅鶴 **29.** flamingo
白鶴 **30.** stork
巢 **31.** nest
長尾雞 **32.** roadrunner

A

B

魚	**A. Fish**	兩棲類、爬蟲類	**B. Amphibians and Reptiles**
海馬	**1.** sea horse	鱷魚	**8.** alligator
鱒魚	**2.** trout	（黃紋）蛇	**9.** (garter) snake
旗魚	**3.** swordfish	響尾蛇	**10.** rattlesnake
尾巴	**a.** tail	眼鏡蛇	**11.** cobra
鰭	**b.** fin	烏龜	**12.** turtle
鰓	**c.** gill	鬣蜥蜴	**13.** iguana
鰻	**4.** eel	火蜥蜴	**14.** salamander
鯊魚	**5.** shark	蜥蜴	**15.** lizard
黃貂魚	**6.** stingray	蝌蚪	**16.** tadpole
比目魚	**7.** flounder	青蛙	**17.** frog
		大龜	**18.** tortoise
		甲殼	**a.** shell

有袋類，無齒類及有翼	**Pouched, Toothless, or Flying Mammals**	小鼠	**9.** mouse
哺乳類		松鼠	**10.** squirrel
無尾熊	**1.** koala	豪豬	**11.** porcupine
穿山甲	**2.** armadillo	豪刺	**a.** quill
袋鼠	**3.** kangaroo	海狸	**12.** beaver
尾巴	**a.** tail	兔	**13.** rabbit
後腿	**b.** hind legs		
袋	**c.** pouch	有蹄哺乳類	**Hoofed Mammals**
前腿	**d.** forelegs	河馬	**14.** hippopotamus
蝙蝠	**4.** bat	美洲駝	**15.** llama
食蟻獸	**5.** anteater	犀牛	**16.** rhinoceros
		角	**a.** horn
齧齒類	**Rodents**	大象	**17.** elephant
花栗鼠	**6.** chipmunk	象鼻	**a.** trunk
大鼠	**7.** rat	象牙	**b.** tusk
土撥鼠	**8.** gopher	斑馬	**18.** zebra

野牛	**19.**	bison	長頸鹿	**29.**	giraffe
小馬	**20.**	pony	豬	**30.**	hog
馬	**21.**	horse	小牛	**31.**	calf
鬃毛		**a.** mane	牛	**32.**	cow
馬仔	**22.**	foal	駱駝	**33.**	camel
驢	**23.**	donkey	駝峯		**a.** hump
小羊	**24.**	lamb	公牛	**34.**	bull
羊	**25.**	sheep	美洲鹿	**35.**	moose
鹿	**26.**	deer	角		**a.** antler
小鹿	**27.**	fawn	蹄		**b.** hoof
山羊	**28.**	goat			

豹子	**1.** leopard
老虎	**2.** tiger
爪子	**a.** claw
獅子	**3.** lion
貓	**4.** cat
小貓	**5.** kitten
狐狸	**6.** fox
浣熊	**7.** raccoon
臭鼬鼠	**8.** skunk

水中哺乳類	**Aquatic Mammals**
鯨魚	**9.** whale
水獺	**10.** otter
海象	**11.** walrus
海豹	**12.** seal
蹼	**a.** flipper
海豚	**13.** dolphin

靈長類		**Primates**	犬		**Dogs**
猴子	**14.**	monkey	長毛狗	**24.**	spaniel
長臂猿	**15.**	gibbon	梗	**25.**	terrier
黑猩猩	**16.**	chimpanzee	獵狗	**26.**	retriever
大猩猩	**17.**	gorilla	小狗	**27.**	puppy
猩猩	**18.**	orangutan	牧羊狗	**28.**	shepherd
狒狒	**19.**	baboon			
			狼	**29.**	wolf
熊		**Bears**	爪	**a.**	paw
大熊貓	**20.**	panda	土狼	**30.**	hyena
黑熊	**21.**	black bear			
北極熊	**22.**	polar bear			
灰熊	**23.**	grizzly bear			

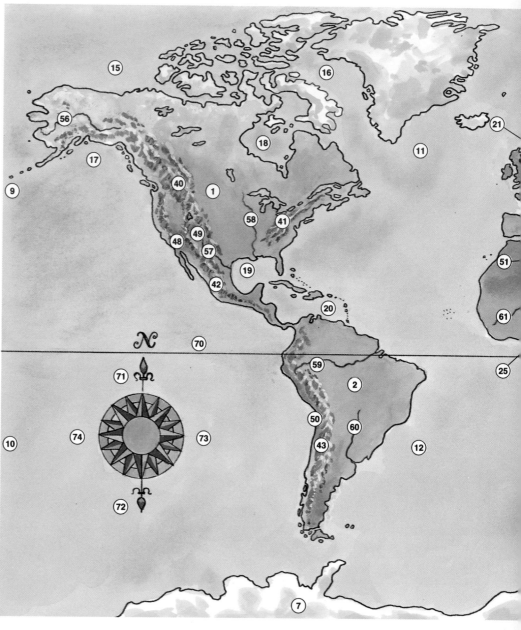

大陸	**Continents**		印度洋	**13.** Indian		黑海	**26.** Black Sea
北美洲	**1.** North America		南冰洋	**14.** Antarctic		裏海	**27.** Caspian Sea
南美洲	**2.** South America					波斯灣	**28.** Persian Gulf
歐洲	**3.** Europe		海，海灣，和小海灣			紅海	**29.** Red Sea
非洲	**4.** Africa			**Seas, Gulfs, and Bays**		阿拉伯海	**30.** Arabian Sea
亞洲	**5.** Asia		波福海	**15.** Beaufort Sea		喀拉海	**31.** Kara Sea
澳洲	**6.** Australia		巴芬灣	**16.** Baffin Bay		孟加拉灣	**32.** Bay of Bengal
南極大陸洲	**7.** Antarctica		阿拉斯加灣	**17.** Gulf of Alaska		拉普提夫海	**33.** Laptev Sea
			哈德遜灣	**18.** Hudson Bay		白令海	**34.** Bering Sea
			墨西哥灣	**19.** Gulf of Mexico		鄂霍次克海	**35.** Sea of Okhotsk
海洋	**Oceans**		加勒比海	**20.** Caribbean Sea		日本海	**36.** Sea of Japan
北冰洋	**8.** Arctic		北海	**21.** North Sea		黃海	**37.** Yellow Sea
北太平洋	**9.** North Pacific		波羅的海	**22.** Baltic Sea		東中國海	**38.** East China Sea
南太平洋	**10.** South Pacific		巴倫支海	**23.** Barents Sea		南中國海	**39.** South China Sea
北大西洋	**11.** North Atlantic		地中海	**24.** Mediterranean Sea			
南大西洋	**12.** South Atlantic		幾內亞灣	**25.** Gulf of Guinea			

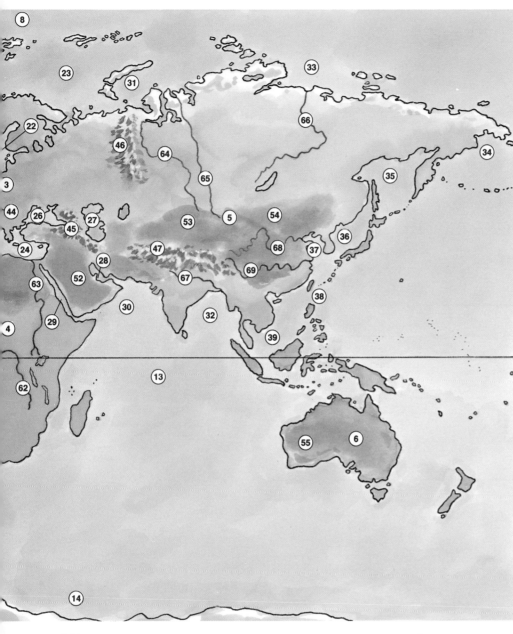

山脈	**Mountain Ranges**
落磯山脈	**40.** Rocky Mountains
阿帕拉契山脈	**41.** Appalachian Mountains
塞拉德雷山脈	**42.** Sierra Madre
安地斯山脈	**43.** Andes
阿爾卑斯山脈	**44.** Alps
高加索山脈	**45.** Caucasus
烏拉山脈	**46.** Urals
喜馬拉雅山脈	**47.** Himalayas

沙漠	**Deserts**
摩哈維沙漠	**48.** Mojave
多色沙漠	**49.** Painted
亞他加馬沙漠	**50.** Atacama

撒哈拉沙漠	**51.** Sahara
拉伯加利大沙漠	**52.** Rub' al Khali
大戈壁沙漠，塔克拉瑪干	**53.** Takla Makan
沙漠	
戈壁沙漠	**54.** Gobi
大沙漠	**55.** Great Sandy

河流	**Rivers**
育康河	**56.** Yukon
里奧格蘭河	**57.** Rio Grande
密西西比河	**58.** Mississippi
亞馬遜河	**59.** Amazon
巴拉那河	**60.** Paraná
尼日河	**61.** Niger

剛果河	**62.** Congo
尼羅河	**63.** Nile
鄂畢河	**64.** Ob
葉尼塞河	**65.** Yenisey
勒拿河	**66.** Lena
恆河	**67.** Ganges
黃河	**68.** Huang
長江	**69.** Yangtze

赤道	**70.** equator
北	**71.** north
南	**72.** south
東	**73.** east
西	**74.** west

阿拉巴馬	**1.** Alabama	印第安納	**14.** Indiana
阿拉斯加	**2.** Alaska	愛阿華	**15.** Iowa
亞利桑那	**3.** Arizona	堪薩斯	**16.** Kansas
阿肯色	**4.** Arkansas	肯塔基	**17.** Kentucky
加利福尼亞	**5.** California	路易西安那	**18.** Louisiana
科羅拉多	**6.** Colorado	緬因	**19.** Maine
康乃狄格	**7.** Connecticut	馬里蘭	**20.** Maryland
德拉瓦	**8.** Delaware	麻薩諸塞	**21.** Massachusetts
佛羅里達	**9.** Florida	密西根	**22.** Michigan
喬治亞	**10.** Georgia	明尼蘇達	**23.** Minnesota
夏威夷	**11.** Hawaii	密西西比	**24.** Mississippi
愛達荷	**12.** Idaho		
伊利諾	**13.** Illinois		

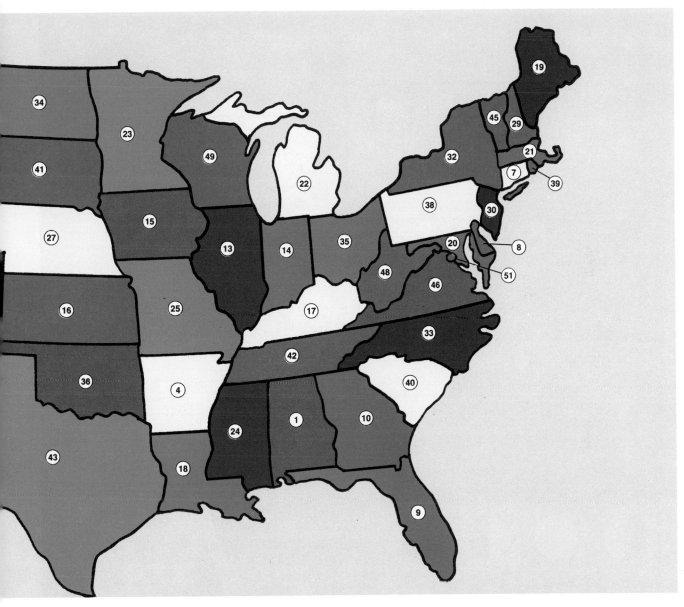

密蘇里	25. Missouri
蒙大那	26. Montana
內布拉斯加	27. Nebraska
內華達	28. Nevada
新罕布夏	29. New Hampshire
新澤西	30. New Jersey
新墨西哥	31. New Mexico
紐約	32. New York
北卡羅來納	33. North Carolina
北達科他	34. North Dakota
俄亥俄	35. Ohio
俄克拉荷馬	36. Oklahoma
俄勒岡	37. Oregon
賓夕法尼亞	38. Pennsylvania

羅得島	39. Rhode Island
南卡羅來納	40. South Carolina
南達科他	41. South Dakota
田納西	42. Tennessee
德克薩斯	43. Texas
猶他	44. Utah
佛蒙特	45. Vermont
維琴尼亞	46. Virginia
華盛頓	47. Washington
西維琴尼亞	48. West Virginia
威斯康辛	49. Wisconsin
懷俄明	50. Wyoming

| 哥倫比亞特區 | 51. District of Columbia |

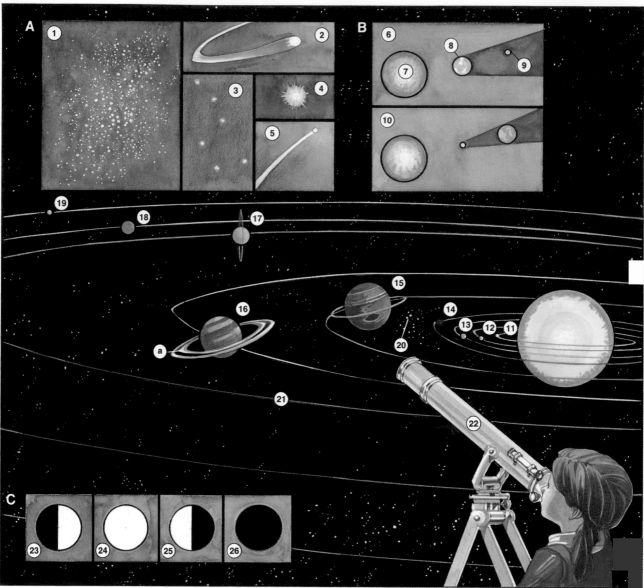

外太空	**A. Outer Space**	火星	**14.** Mars
銀河系	**1.** galaxy	木星	**15.** Jupiter
彗星	**2.** comet	土星	**16.** Saturn
（北斗七星）星座	**3.** (Big Dipper) constellation	光環	**a.** ring
恆星	**4.** star	天王星	**17.** Uranus
流星	**5.** meteor	海王星	**18.** Neptune
		冥王星	**19.** Pluto
太陽系	**B. The Solar System**		
月蝕	**6.** lunar eclipse	小遊星	**20.** asteroid
太陽	**7.** Sun	軌道	**21.** orbit
地球	**8.** Earth	望遠鏡	**22.** telescope
月球	**9.** Moon		
日蝕	**10.** solar eclipse	月象	**C. Phases of the Moon**
		上弦月	**23.** first quarter
行星	*The Planets*	滿月	**24.** full moon
水星	**11.** Mercury	下弦月	**25.** last quarter
金星	**12.** Venus	新月	**26.** new moon
地球	**13.** Earth		

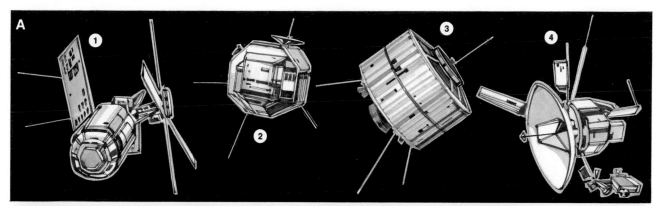

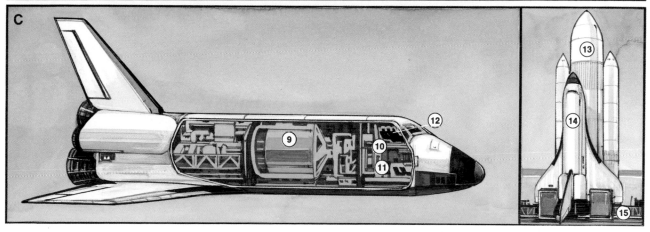

太空船	**A. Spacecraft**	航天飛機，太空梭	**C. The Space Shuttle**
太空站	**1.** space station	貨艙	**9.** cargo bay
通訊衛星	**2.** communication satellite	儀器艙	**10.** flight deck
氣象衛星	**3.** weather satellite	生活區	**11.** living quarters
太空探測火箭	**4.** space probe	乘員	**12.** crew
		火箭發動機	**13.** rocket
登陸月球	**B. Landing on the Moon**	航天飛機，太空梭	**14.** space shuttle
太空人	**5.** astronaut	發射臺	**15.** launchpad
太空衣	**6.** space suit		
登月小艇	**7.** lunar module		
指揮艙	**8.** command module		

旗	**1.** flag		彈簧筆記本	**15.** spiral notebook
鐘	**2.** clock		書桌	**16.** desk
擴音器	**3.** loudspeaker		膠水	**17.** glue
老師	**4.** teacher		刷	**18.** brush
黑板	**5.** chalkboard		學生	**19.** student
衣箱	**6.** locker		削鉛筆刀	**20.** pencil sharpener
佈告版	**7.** bulletin board		橡皮	**21.** pencil eraser
電腦，計算機	**8.** computer		原子筆	**22.** ballpoint pen
粉筆溝	**9.** chalk tray		尺	**23.** ruler
粉筆	**10.** chalk		鉛筆	**24.** pencil
黑板擦	**11.** eraser		圖釘	**25.** thumbtack
走廊	**12.** hall		教科書	**26.** (text)book
活頁紙	**13.** (loose-leaf) paper		投影機	**27.** overhead projector
活頁夾	**14.** ring binder			

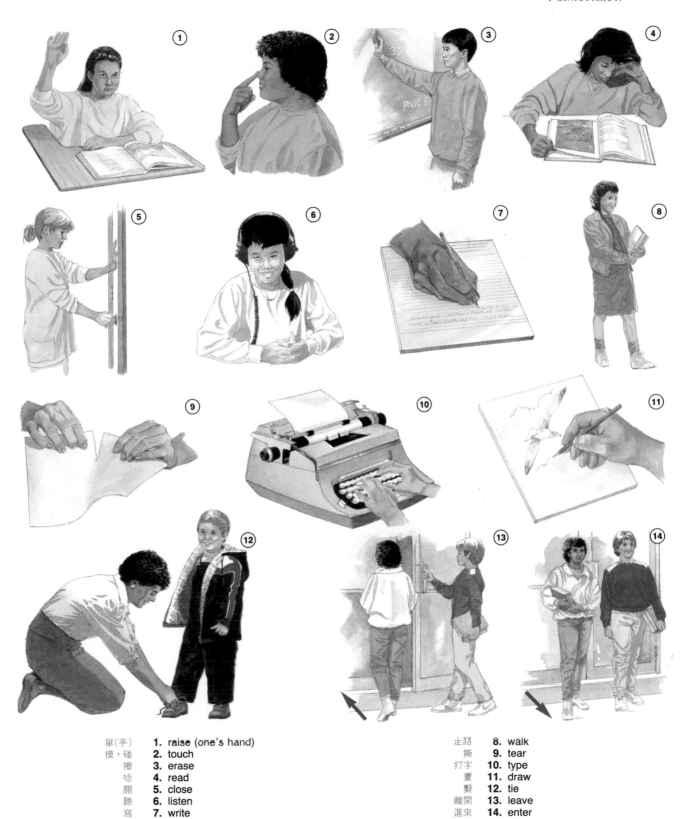

舉(手)	**1.** raise (one's hand)
摸，碰	**2.** touch
擦	**3.** erase
唸	**4.** read
關	**5.** close
聽	**6.** listen
寫	**7.** write

走路	**8.** walk
撕	**9.** tear
打字	**10.** type
畫	**11.** draw
繫	**12.** tie
離開	**13.** leave
進來	**14.** enter

棱鏡	**1.** prism	橡皮管	**18.** rubber tubing
三角瓶	**2.** flask	環架	**19.** ring stand
培養皿	**3.** petri dish	煤氣燈，本生燈	**20.** Bunsen burner
秤	**4.** scale	火焰	**21.** flame
秤鉈，法碼	**5.** weights	溫度計	**22.** thermometer
鐵紗網	**6.** wire mesh screen	燒杯	**23.** beaker
夾	**7.** clamp	工作台	**24.** bench
試管架	**8.** rack	量筒	**25.** graduated cylinder
試管	**9.** test tube	滴管	**26.** medicine dropper
管塞	**10.** stopper	磁鐵	**27.** magnet
作圖紙	**11.** graph paper	鉗子	**28.** forceps
護目鏡	**12.** safety glasses	火鉗	**29.** tongs
計時器	**13.** timer	顯微鏡	**30.** microscope
移液管	**14.** pipette	玻片	**31.** slide
放大鏡	**15.** magnifying glass	鑷子	**32.** tweezers
濾紙	**16.** filter paper	解剖工具	**33.** dissection kit
漏斗	**17.** funnel	圓形凳	**34.** stool

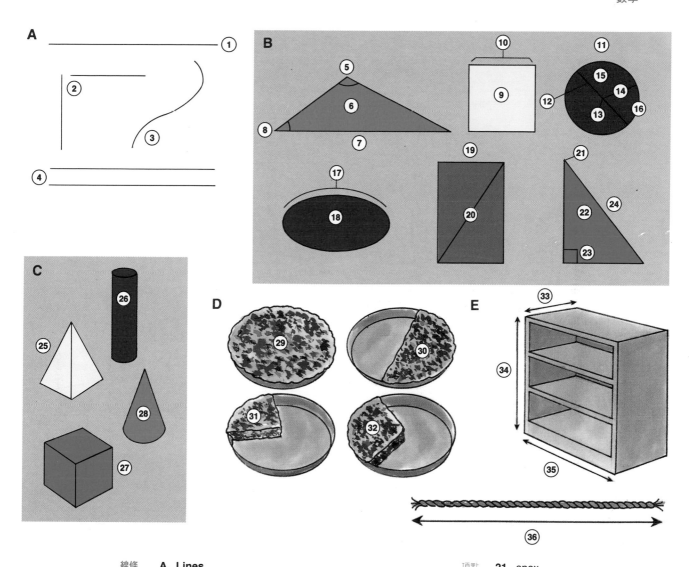

線條	**A. Lines**		頂點	**21.** apex
直線	**1.** straight line		直角三角形	**22.** right triangle
垂直線	**2.** perpendicular lines		直角	**23.** right angle
曲線	**3.** curve		斜邊	**24.** hypotenuse
平行線	**4.** parallel lines			

幾何圖形	**B. Geometrical Figures**		立體圖形	**C. Solid Figures**
鈍角	**5.** obtuse angle		角錐	**25.** pyramid
三角形	**6.** triangle		圓柱	**26.** cylinder
底邊	**7.** base		立方體	**27.** cube
銳角	**8.** acute angle		圓錐	**28.** cone
方形	**9.** square			
邊	**10.** side		分數	**D. Fractions**
圓形	**11.** circle		整體	**29.** whole
直徑	**12.** diameter		一半，二分之一	**30.** a half ($\frac{1}{2}$)
圓心	**13.** center		四分之一	**31.** a quarter ($\frac{1}{4}$)
半徑	**14.** radius		三分之一	**32.** a third ($\frac{1}{3}$)
區域	**15.** section			
弧	**16.** arc		測量	**E. Measurement**
周長	**17.** circumference		深	**33.** depth
橢圓形	**18.** oval		高	**34.** height
長方形	**19.** rectangle		寬	**35.** width
對角線	**20.** diagonal		長	**36.** length

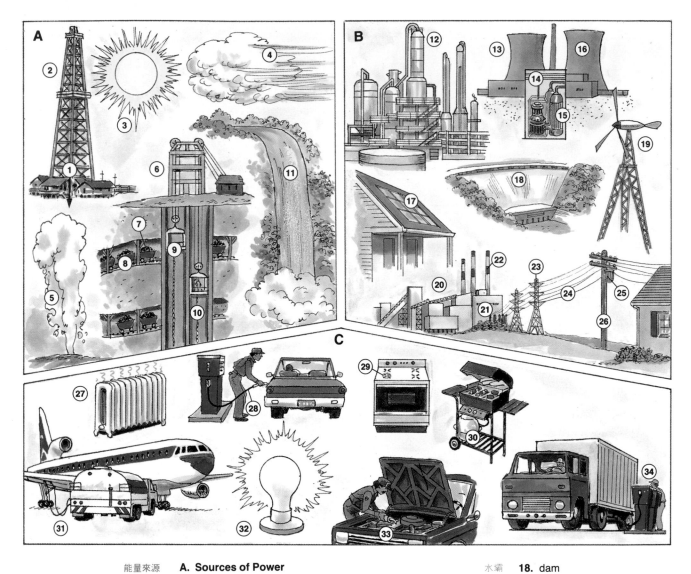

能量來源	**A. Sources of Power**		水壩	18. dam
油井	1. oil well		風車	19. windmill
井架	2. derrick		發電站	20. power station
太陽	3. sun		發電機	21. electrical generator
風	4. wind		煙窗	22. smokestack
噴泉	5. geyser		輸電塔	23. transmission towers
煤礦	6. coal mine		高壓輸電線	24. power lines
煤	7. coal		變壓器	25. transformer
井下煤車	8. shuttle		電柱	26. utility pole
電梯	9. elevator			
電梯道，豎坑	10. shaft		應用及產品	**C. Uses and Products**
瀑布	11. waterfall		熱	27. heat
			石油	28. gas(oline)
能量生成	**B. Generation of Power**		天然瓦斯	29. natural gas
煉油廠	12. refinery		丙烷氣體	30. propane gas
核反應爐	13. nuclear reactor		航空燃油	31. jet fuel
堆蕊	14. core		電	32. electricity
鈾柱	15. uranium rods		機油	33. motor oil
冷却塔	16. cooling tower		柴油	34. diesel fuel
日光收集板	17. solar collector			

酪農場	**A. Dairy Farm**		草叉	14. pitchfork
果園	1. orchard		拖拉機	15. tractor
果樹	2. fruit tree		麥田	16. (wheat) field
農家	3. farmhouse		聯合收割機	17. combine
秣草貯藏室	4. silo		排	18. row
穀倉	5. barn		稻草人	19. scarecrow
牧草地	6. pasture			
農人	7. farmer		牧場	**C. Ranch**
穀倉近旁的空地	8. barnyard		牛(羣)	20. (herd of) cattle
柵欄	9. fence		牧牛仔	21. cowboy
羊	10. sheep		牧牛女	22. cowgirl
乳牛	11. dairy cow		馬	23. horses
			畜欄	24. corral
麥場	**B. Wheat Farm**		細長馬槽	25. trough
家畜	12. livestock			
乾草(堆)	13. (bale of) hay			

工地	**A. Construction Site**		鏟子	15. shovel
椽	1. rafters		木板	16. board
木瓦	2. shingle		接線工	17. linesman
水平尺	3. level		升降車	18. cherry picker
安全帽	4. hard hat			
技術員	5. builder		道路施工	**B. Road Work**
藍圖	6. blueprints		指示錐	19. cone
鷹架	7. scaffolding		旗子	20. flag
梯子	8. ladder		路障	21. barricade
腳蹬橫木	9. rung		風鎬	22. jackhammer
水泥	10. cement		獨輪車	23. wheelbarrow
地基	11. foundation		分向胸牆	24. center divider
磚	12. bricks		水泥攪拌車	25. cement mixer
鶴嘴鋤，十字架	13. pickax		堆土機	26. backhoe
建築工	14. construction worker		壓路機	27. bulldozer

交換臺接線員	**1.**	switchboard operator
通話器	**2.**	headset
交換臺	**3.**	switchboard
打印機	**4.**	printer
隔間	**5.**	cubicle
打字員	**6.**	typist
文字處理機	**7.**	word processor
電腦輸出紙	**8.**	printout
月曆	**9.**	calendar
打字機	**10.**	typewriter
秘書	**11.**	secretary
文件架框	**12.**	in-box
書桌	**13.**	desk
環形索引夾	**14.**	rolodex
電話	**15.**	telephone
電腦，計算機	**16.**	computer
打字椅	**17.**	typing chair
經理	**18.**	manager
計算器	**19.**	calculator
書架	**20.**	bookcase
檔案櫃	**21.**	file cabinet
檔案夾	**22.**	file folder
文件管理員	**23.**	file clerk
影印機	**24.**	photocopier
留言簿	**25.**	message pad
便箋	**26.**	(legal) pad
釘書機	**27.**	stapler
廻紋針	**28.**	paper clips
起釘書針夾	**29.**	staple remover
削鉛筆機	**30.**	pencil sharpener
信封	**31.**	envelope

藥技師	**1.** pharmacist	烘麵包師	**8.** baker
技師	**2.** mechanic	眼鏡商	**9.** optician
理髮師	**3.** barber	美容師	**10.** hairdresser
旅遊代辦人	**4.** travel agent	花商	**11.** florist
修理工	**5.** repairperson	珠寶商	**12.** jeweller
裁縫	**6.** tailor	肉販	**13.** butcher
水果店主	**7.** greengrocer		

維修	**A. Repair and Maintenance**
水管工	1. plumber
木匠	2. carpenter
花匠	3. gardener
鎖匠	4. locksmith
房地產代理商	5. real estate agent
電工	6. electrician
油漆工	7. painter

家庭幫工	**B. Household Services**
管家	8. housekeeper
清潔工	9. janitor
送貨人	10. delivery boy
門房	11. doorman

工廠工作	**C. Factory Work**
工人	12. shop worker
監工	13. foreman

媒體及藝術	**A. Media and Arts**
氣象播報員	**1.** weather forecaster
新聞播報員	**2.** newscaster
藝術家	**3.** artist
攝影家	**4.** photographer
模特兒	**5.** model
服裝設計師	**6.** fashion designer
作家	**7.** writer
建築師	**8.** architect
音樂節目主持人	**9.** disc jockey (DJ)
攝影記者	**10.** cameraperson
記者	**11.** reporter
推銷員	**12.** salesperson

銀行業	**B. Banking**
主管	**13.** officer
警衛	**14.** security guard
出納員	**15.** teller

商業服務人員	**C. Business Workers**
電腦程式員	**16.** computer programmer
招待員	**17.** receptionist
會計	**18.** accountant
信差	**19.** messenger

動物園	**1.** zoo		垃圾桶	**11.** trash can
樂隊演奏場	**2.** band shell		滑梯	**12.** slide
小販	**3.** vendor		沙盒	**13.** sandbox
手推貨車	**4.** hand truck		噴水器	**14.** sprinkler
旋轉木馬	**5.** merry-go-round		遊戲場	**15.** playground
騎馬者	**6.** horseback rider		鞦韆	**16.** swings
騎馬道	**7.** bridle path		立體方格架	**17.** jungle gym
（鴨）池	**8.** (duck) pond		蹺蹺板	**18.** seesaw
慢跑跑道	**9.** jogging path		飲用噴泉	**19.** water fountain
長椅	**10.** bench			

高原，高地	**1.** plateau
徒步旅行者	**2.** hikers
峽谷	**3.** canyon
丘陵，小山	**4.** hill
公園警衛	**5.** park ranger

	Fishing
釣魚	
小溪	**6.** stream
釣魚竿	**7.** fishing rod
釣魚線	**8.** fishing line
魚網	**9.** fishing net
釣魚用防水長靴	**10.** waders
岩石	**11.** rocks

野餐區	**Picnic Area**
烤架	**12.** grill
野餐籃	**13.** picnic basket
熱水瓶	**14.** thermos
野餐臺	**15.** picnic table

划筏		**Rafting**
筏	**16.**	raft
急流	**17.**	rapids
瀑布	**18.**	waterfall
爬山		**Mountain Climbing**
山	**19.**	mountain
頂峯	**20.**	peak
懸崖	**21.**	cliff
背負皮帶	**22.**	harness
繩子	**23.**	rope

露營		**Camping**
帳蓬	**24.**	tent
野營爐	**25.**	camp stove
睡袋	**26.**	sleeping bag
裝具	**27.**	gear
背包架	**28.**	frame backpack
提燈	**29.**	lantern
椿	**30.**	stake
營火	**31.**	campfire
樹林	**32.**	woods

海濱板道	**1.** boardwalk
點心亭	**2.** refreshment stand
汽車旅館	**3.** motel
騎自行車者	**4.** biker
口哨	**5.** whistle
救生員	**6.** lifeguard
雙筒望遠鏡	**7.** binoculars
救生椅	**8.** lifeguard chair
救生圈	**9.** life preserver
救生艇	**10.** lifeboat
塑料充氣球	**11.** beach ball

沙丘	**12.** sand dunes
飛盤	**13.** Frisbee™
太陽眼鏡	**14.** sunglasses
浴巾	**15.** beach towel
桶	**16.** pail
鏟子	**17.** shovel
游泳衣	**18.** bathing suit
日光浴者	**19.** sunbather
海濱椅	**20.** beach chair
海濱太陽傘	**21.** beach umbrella

風箏	**22.** kite	沙堆堡	**32.** sandcastle
跑步者	**23.** runners	游泳褲	**33.** bathing trunks
波浪	**24.** wave	潛水鏡	**34.** snorkel
衝浪板	**25.** surfboard	潛水面具	**35.** mask
充氣墊	**26.** air mattress	蛙人脚	**36.** flippers
浮墊(練習踢脚用的木板)	**27.** kickboard	氧氣瓶	**37.** scuba tank
游泳者	**28.** swimmer	潛水面具	**38.** wet suit
充氣胎	**29.** tube	防晒油	**39.** suntan lotion
水	**30.** water	貝殻	**40.** shell
沙	**31.** sand	冰盒	**41.** cooler

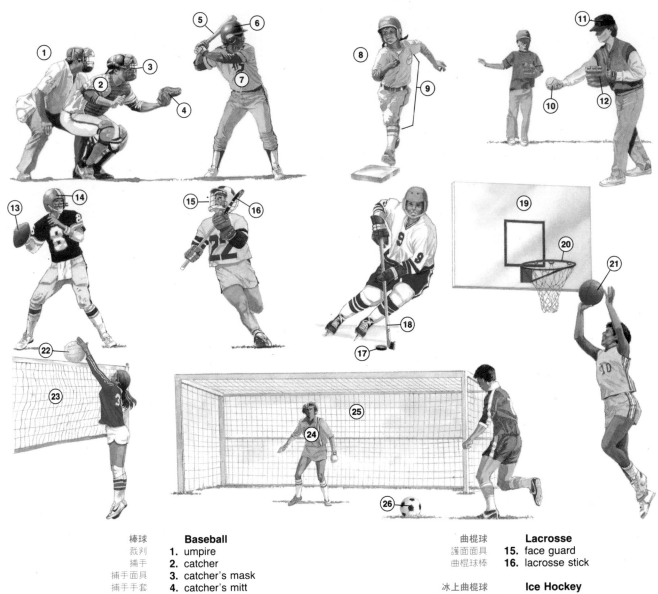

棒球 | **Baseball**
裁判 | **1.** umpire
捕手 | **2.** catcher
捕手面具 | **3.** catcher's mask
捕手手套 | **4.** catcher's mitt
棒球棒 | **5.** bat
棒球球盔 | **6.** batting helmet
打擊手 | **7.** batter

少年棒球 | **Little League Baseball**
少棒球員 | **8.** Little Leaguer
制服 | **9.** uniform

壘球 | **Softball**
壘球 | **10.** softball
球帽 | **11.** cap
手套 | **12.** glove

美式足球 | **Football**
足球 | **13.** football
頭盔 | **14.** helmet

曲棍球 | **Lacrosse**
護面面具 | **15.** face guard
曲棍球棒 | **16.** lacrosse stick

冰上曲棍球 | **Ice Hockey**
冰球 | **17.** puck
冰球桿 | **18.** hockey stick

籃球 | **Basketball**
球板 | **19.** backboard
籃 | **20.** basket
籃球 | **21.** basketball

排球 | **Volleyball**
排球 | **22.** volleyball
網 | **23.** net

足球 | **Soccer**
守門員 | **24.** goalie
球門 | **25.** goal
足球 | **26.** soccer ball

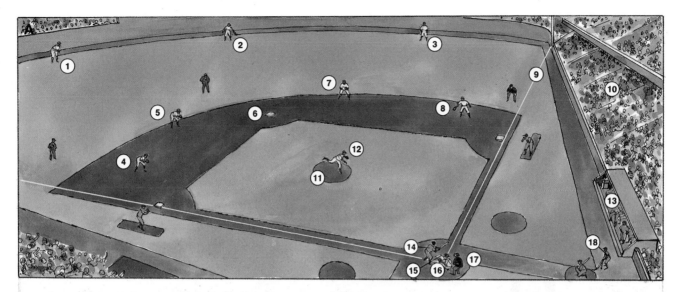

棒球場	**A. Baseball Diamond**	足球場	**B. Football Field**
左外野手	**1.** left fielder	計分板	**19.** scoreboard
中堅手	**2.** center fielder	啦啦隊隊長	**20.** cheerleaders
右外野手	**3.** right fielder	敎練	**21.** coach
三壘手	**4.** third baseman	裁判	**22.** referee
游擊手	**5.** shortstop	終點區	**23.** end zone
壘	**6.** base	左衛	**24.** split end
二壘手	**7.** second baseman	左外鋒	**25.** left tackle
一壘手	**8.** first baseman	左內鋒	**26.** left guard
邊線	**9.** foul line	中鋒	**27.** center
看臺	**10.** stands	右內鋒	**28.** right guard
投手周圍隆起的小丘	**11.** pitcher's mound	右外鋒	**29.** right tackle
投手	**12.** pitcher	右衛	**30.** tight end
選手休息室	**13.** dugout	側衛	**31.** flanker
打擊手	**14.** batter	四分後衛	**32.** quarterback
本壘	**15.** home plate	前衛	**33.** halfback
捕手	**16.** catcher	後衛	**34.** fullback
裁判	**17.** umpire	門柱	**35.** goalpost
棒球球童	**18.** batboy		

網球	**Tennis**
網球	1. tennis ball
網球拍	2. racket

保齡球	**Bowling**
溝	3. gutter
道	4. lane
保齡球瓶	5. pin
保齡球	6. bowling ball

高爾夫球	**Golf**
高爾夫球	7. golf ball
洞	8. hole
推棒	9. putter
高爾夫球員	10. golfer

手球	**Handball**
手套	11. glove
手球	12. handball
球場	13. court

拳擊	**Boxing**
護頭	14. head protector
手套	15. glove
裁判	16. referee
拳擊場	17. ring

乒乓球	**Ping-Pong**
乒乓球拍	18. paddle
乒乓球	19. ping-pong ball

賽馬	**Horse Racing**
馬鞍	20. saddle
賽馬師	21. jockey
韁繩	22. reins

體操	**Gymnastics**
體操運動員	23. gymnast
平衡木	24. balance beam

溜冰	**Ice Skating**
冰場	25. rink
冰鞋	26. skate
冰刀	27. blade

球拍	**Racquetball**
護目	28. safety goggles
球拍	29. racquet
拍球	30. racquetball

田徑	**Track and Field**
跑步運動員，跑步者	31. runner
跑道	32. track

越野滑雪	**Cross-Country Skiing**
滑雪板	33. skis
雪杖	34. pole
滑雪的人，滑雪運動員	35. skier

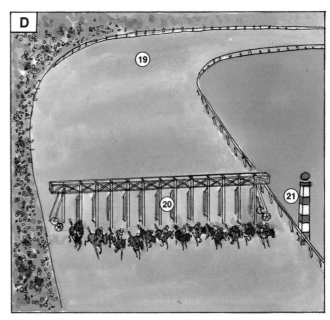

網球場	**A. Tennis Court**
發球落區	**1.** service court
球網	**2.** net
發球線	**3.** service line
底線	**4.** baseline

高爾夫球場	**B. Golf Course**
高爾夫球桿	**5.** clubs
高爾夫球場草地	**6.** rough
高爾夫球桿袋	**7.** golf bag
高爾夫球車	**8.** golf cart
旗	**9.** flag
果嶺	**10.** green
沙障	**11.** sand trap
高爾夫球場整修過的草地	**12.** fairway
球座	**13.** tee

滑雪坡	**C. Ski Slope**
滑雪杖	**14.** pole
滑雪靴	**15.** ski boot
脚卡	**16.** binding
滑雪板	**17.** ski
滑雪吊車	**18.** ski lift

賽馬道	**D. Race Track**
賽馬跑道	**19.** stretch
起跑門	**20.** starting gate
終線	**21.** finish line

打	1. hit
發	2. serve
踢	3. kick
接	4. catch

傳	5. pass
跑	6. run
跌倒	7. fall
跳	8. jump

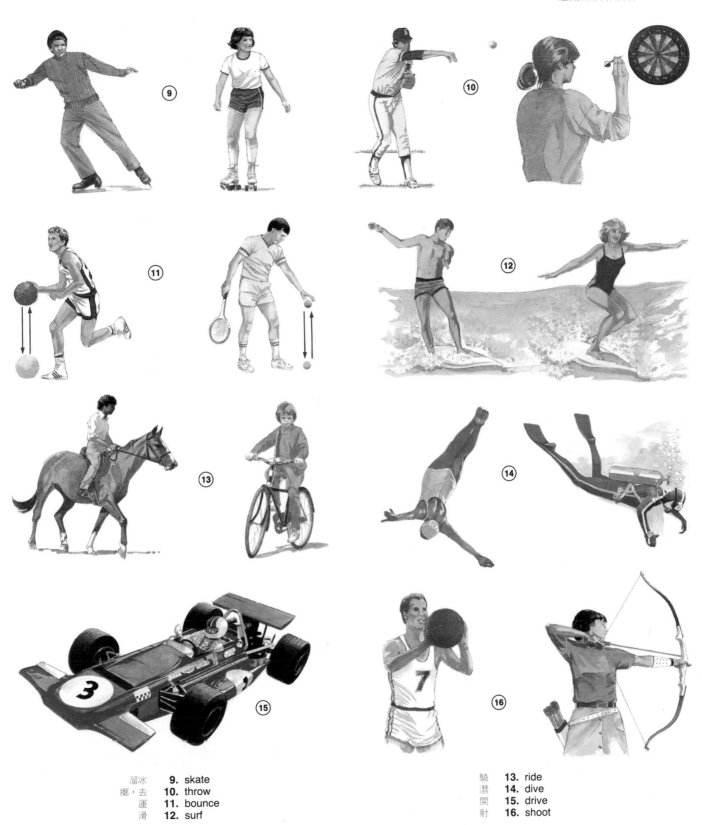

溜冰　　**9.** skate
擲，去　**10.** throw
運　　　**11.** bounce
滑　　　**12.** surf

騎　**13.** ride
潛　**14.** dive
開　**15.** drive
射　**16.** shoot

弦樂器	**Strings**
鋼琴	**1.** piano
琴鍵盤	**a.** keyboard
樂譜	**2.** sheet music
四弦琴	**3.** ukulele
曼陀淋	**4.** mandolin
五弦琴	**5.** banjo
豎琴	**6.** harp
小提琴	**7.** violin
弓	**a.** bow
中提琴	**8.** viola
大提琴	**9.** cello
低音提琴	**10.** bass
弦	**a.** string
吉他	**11.** guitar
彈片	**a.** pick

木管樂器	**Woodwinds**
高音笛	**12.** piccolo
橫笛	**13.** flute
低音簧	**14.** bassoon
雙簧管	**15.** oboe
單簧管	**16.** clarinet

打擊樂器	**Percussion**
法國擊鼓	**17.** tambourine
鐃鈸	**18.** cymbals
鼓	**19.** drum
鼓捶	**a.** drumsticks
康茄鼓	**20.** conga
半球形銅鼓	**21.** kettledrum
(古巴)小鼓	**22.** bongos

銅管樂器	**Brass**
伸縮喇叭	**23.** trombone
薩克斯風	**24.** saxophone
喇叭	**25.** trumpet
法國號	**26.** French horn
低音喇叭	**27.** tuba

其他樂器	**Other Instruments**
手風琴	**28.** accordion
風琴	**29.** organ
口琴	**30.** harmonica
木琴	**31.** xylophone

芭蕾	**A. The Ballet**
戲幕	**1.** curtain
場景	**2.** scenery
舞者	**3.** dancer
追光	**4.** spotlight
舞臺	**5.** stage
樂隊	**6.** orchestra
指揮臺	**7.** podium
指揮	**8.** conductor
指揮棒	**9.** baton
音樂家	**10.** musician
包廂位	**11.** box seat
場座	**12.** orchestra seating
樓座	**13.** mezzanine
包廂	**14.** balcony
聽眾，觀眾	**15.** audience
引座員	**16.** usher
節目單	**17.** programs

喜歌劇	**B. Musical Comedy**
合唱	**18.** chorus
男演員	**19.** actor
女演員	**20.** actress

搖滾樂隊	**C. Rock Group**
音響合成器	**21.** synthesizer
電子琴手	**22.** keyboard player
低音吉他手	**23.** bass guitarist
歌者	**24.** singer
主吉他手	**25.** lead guitarist
電吉他	**26.** electric guitar
鼓手	**27.** drummer

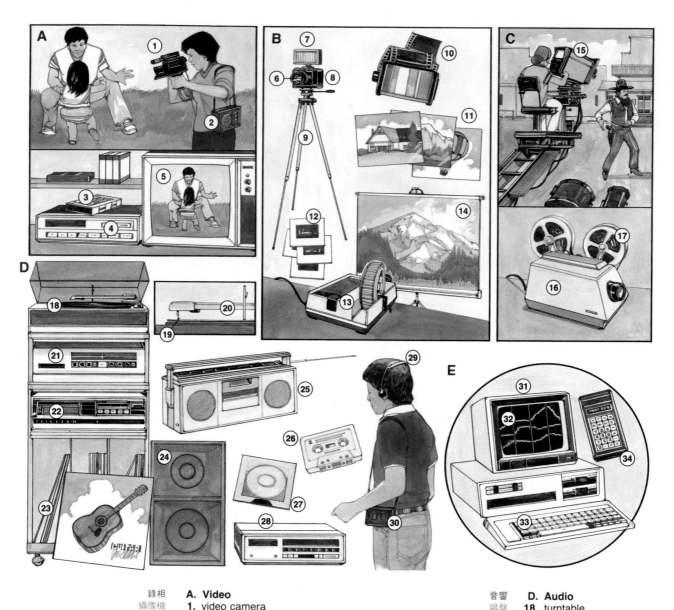

錄相	**A. Video**		音響	**D. Audio**
攝像機	**1.** video camera		唱盤	**18.** turntable
手提式錄相機	**2.** Minicam™		唱針	**19.** cartridge needle
錄影帶	**3.** videocassette (tape)		唱臂	**20.** arm
錄放影機	**4.** VCR (videocassette recorder)		接收器	**21.** receiver
電視	**5.** television		錄音部分	**22.** cassette deck
			唱片	**23.** records
照相	**B. Photography**		喇叭	**24.** speaker
鏡頭	**6.** lens		立體聲錄音帶	**25.** stereo cassette player
閃光燈	**7.** flash		錄音帶，錄音磁帶	**26.** cassette
照相機	**8.** camera		激光唱片	**27.** compact disc (CD)
三角架	**9.** tripod		激光唱機	**28.** compact disc player
膠卷	**10.** (roll of) film		耳機	**29.** headphones
相片	**11.** prints		新力牌隨身聽	**30.** Sony Walkman
幻燈片	**12.** slides			
幻燈機	**13.** slide projector		電腦，計算機	**E. Computer**
銀幕	**14.** screen		個人電腦	**31.** personal computer (PC)
			電腦屏幕	**32.** monitor
電影	**C. Film**		鍵盤	**33.** keyboard
攝影機	**15.** movie camera		計算器	**34.** calculator
放映機	**16.** projector			
電影膠卷	**17.** (reel of) film			

縫紉	**A. Sewing**
縫紉機	**1.** sewing machine
線（卷）	**2.** (spool of) thread
針墊	**3.** pincushion
材料	**4.** material
裁縫剪	**5.** pinking shears
樣片	**6.** pattern piece
款式，花樣	**7.** pattern
鈕鈕洞	**8.** buttonhole
鈕鈕	**9.** button
縫合線	**10.** seam
縫邊	**11.** hem
襯邊	**12.** hem binding
按鈕	**13.** snap
鈎和鈎掛	**14.** hook and eye
皮尺	**15.** tape measure
拉鍊	**16.** zipper
（一把）剪刀	**17.** (pair of) scissors

針	**18.** needle
縫針，針脚	**19.** stitch
大頭針	**20.** pin
頂針	**21.** thimble
其他針織、縫紉用品	**B. Other Needlecrafts**
編織	**22.** knitting
毛線	**23.** wool
線軸	**24.** skein
毛線針	**25.** knitting needle
針織花邊	**26.** needlepoint
刺綉	**27.** embroidery
鈎製品	**28.** crochet
鈎針	**29.** crochet hook
織	**30.** weaving
紗，線	**31.** yarn
拼縫	**32.** quilting

在(窗口)	**1.** at (the window)	在(抽屜)裡	**7.** in (the drawer)
在(黑貓)之上	**2.** above (the black cat)	在(書桌)之下	**8.** under (the desk)
在(白貓)之下	**3.** below (the white cat)	在(椅子)後	**9.** behind (the chair)
在(枕頭)之間	**4.** between (the pillows)	在(桌)上	**10.** on top of (the table)
在(地毯)上	**5.** on (the rug)	在(電視機)旁邊	**11.** next to (the TV)
在(壁爐)前	**6.** in front of (the fireplace)		

穿過(燈塔)	**1.** through (the lighthouse)
繞過(燈塔)	**2.** around (the lighthouse)
下(坡)	**3.** down (the hill)
向着(球洞)	**4.** toward (the hole)
離開(球洞)	**5.** away from (the hole)
越過(水塘)	**6.** across (the water)

出(水)	**7.** out of (the water)
過(橋)	**8.** over (the bridge)
朝向(球場)	**9.** to (the course)
從(球場)來	**10.** from (the course)
上(坡)	**11.** up (the hill)
進(球洞)	**12.** into (the hole)

星期中的各天	**Days of the Week**
星期日	Sunday
星期一	Monday
星期二	Tuesday
星期三	Wednesday
星期四	Thursday
星期五	Friday
星期六	Saturday

月份	**Months of the Year**
一月	January
二月	February
三月	March
四月	April
五月	May
六月	June
七月	July
八月	August
九月	September
十月	October
十一月	November
十二月	December

數字	**Numbers**
零	0 zero
一	1 one
二	2 two
三	3 three
四	4 four
五	5 five
六	6 six
七	7 seven
八	8 eight
九	9 nine
十	10 ten
十一	11 eleven
十二	12 twelve
十三	13 thirteen
十四	14 fourteen
十五	15 fifteen
十六	16 sixteen
十七	17 seventeen
十八	18 eighteen
十九	19 nineteen
二十	20 twenty
二十一	21 twenty-one
三十	30 thirty
四十	40 forty
五十	50 fifty
六十	60 sixty
七十	70 seventy
八十	80 eighty
九十	90 ninety
一百	100 a/one hundred
五百	500 five hundred
六百二十一	621 six hundred (and) twenty-one
一千	1,000 a/one thousand
一百萬	1,000,000 a/one million

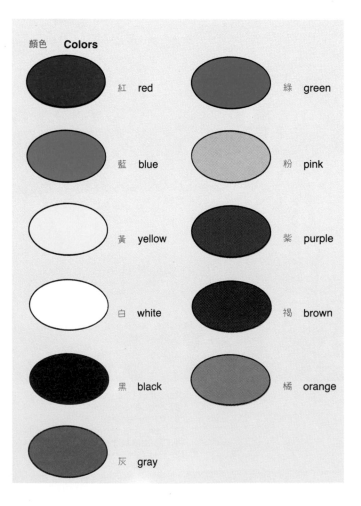

顏色 Colors

紅 red	綠 green
藍 blue	粉 pink
黃 yellow	紫 purple
白 white	褐 brown
黑 black	橘 orange
灰 gray	

Two numbers occur after words in the index: the first refers to the page where the word is illustrated and the second to the item number of the word on that page. For example, above [ə bŭv╱] **102** 2 means that the word *above* is the item numbered 2 on page 102. If only a bold number appears, then that word is part of the unit title or a subtitle.

The index includes a pronunciation guide for all the words illustrated in the book. This guide uses symbols commonly found in dictionaries for native speakers. These symbols, unlike those used in transcription systems such as the International Phonetic Alphabet, tend to preserve spelling and so should help you to become more aware of the connections between written English and spoken English.

Consonants

[b] as in **back** [băk] [k] as in **kite** [kīt] [sh] as in **shell** [shĕl]
[ch] as in **cheek** [chēk] [l] as in **leaf** [lēf] [t] as in **tape** [tāp]
[d] as in **date** [dāt] [m] as in **man** [măn] [th] as in **three** [thrē]
[dh] as in **the** [dh] [n] as in **neck** [nĕk] [v] as in **vine** [vīn]
[f] as in **face** [fās] [ng] as in **ring** [rĭng] [w] as in **waist** [wāst]
[g] as in **gas** [găs] [p] as in **pack** [păk] [y] as in **yam** [yăm]
[h] as in **half** [hăf] [r] as in **rake** [rāk] [z] as in **zoo** [zoo]
[j] as in **jack** [jăk] [s] as in **sand** [sănd] [zh] as in **measure** [mĕzh╱ər]

Vowels

[ā] as in **bake** [bāk] [ī] as in **lime** [līm] [oo] as in **cool** [kool]
[ă] as in **back** [băk] [ĭ] as in **lip** [lĭp] [ŏŏ] as in **book** [bŏŏk]
[ä] as in **bar** [bär] [ï] as in **beer** [bïr] [ow] as in **cow** [kow]
[ē] as in **beat** [bēt] [ō] as in **post** [pōst] [oy] as in **boy** [boy]
[ĕ] as in **bed** [bĕd] [ŏ] as in **box** [bŏks] [ŭ] as in **cut** [kŭt]
[ë] as in **bear** [bër] [ö] as in **claw** [klö] [ü] as in **curb** [kürb]
    or **for** [för] [ə] as in **above** [ə bŭv╱]

All pronunciation symbols used are alphabetical except for the schwa [ə], which is the most frequent vowel sound in English. If you use it appropriately in unstressed syllables, your pronunciation will sound more natural.

You should note that an umlaut ([¨]) calls attention to the special quality of vowels before [r]. (The sound [ö] can also represent a vowel not followed by [r] as in *claw.*) You should listen carefully to native speakers to discover how these vowels actually sound.

Stress

This guide also follows the system for marking stress used in many dictionaries for native speakers.
    (1) Stress is not marked if a word consisting of a single syllable occurs in isolation.
    (2) Where stress is marked, two levels are distinguished:
        a bold accent [╱] is placed after each syllable with primary stress,
        a light accent [╱] is placed after each syllable with secondary stress.

Syllable Boundaries

Syllable boundaries are indicated by a single space.

NOTE: The pronunciation used in this index is based on patterns of American English. There has been no attempt to represent all of the varieties of American English. Students should listen to native speakers to hear how the language actually sounds in a particular region.

above [ə bŭv′] **102** 2

abdomen [ăb′də mən] **4** 14

accelerator [ăk sĕl′ə rā′tər] **50** 27

accordion [ə kör′dē ən] **98** 28

accountant [ə kown′tənt] **86** 18

acorn [ā′körn] **61** 33b

acorn squash [ā′körn skwŏsh′] **7** 28

across [ə krös′] **103** 6

actor [ăk′tər] **99** 19

actress [ăk′trəs] **99** 20

acute angle [ə kyoot′ăng′gəl] **79** 8

address [ă′drĕs] **46** 11

adjectives [ăj′ĭk tĭvz] **24, 25**

aerial tramway [ër′ē əl trăm′wā] **55** 31

Africa [ă′frĭ kə] **70** 4

after-shave lotion [ăf′tər shāv lō′shən]
    23 21

ailments [āl′mənts] **40**

air conditioner [ër′kən dĭ′shə nər]
    32 11

air filter [ër′fĭl′tər] **51** 52

Air Force [ër′förs′] **48** 19

air mattress [ër′mă′trəs] **91** 26

air pump [ër′pŭmp′] **53** 13

air travel [ër′tră′vəl] **56**

aircraft [ër′krăft′] **57**

aircraft carrier [ër′krăft kăr′yər] **48** 4

aircraft types [ër′krăft tīps′] **57**

(airmail) envelope
    [ër′māl ĕn′və lōp] **46** 16

airman [ër′mən] **48** 20

airport check-in [ër′pört chĕk′ĭn] **56**

aisle [ī′əl] **14** 10, **56** 23

Alabama [ăl′ə bă′mə] **72** 1

alarm clock [ə lärm′klŏk] **32** 8

Alaska [ə lăs′kə] **72** 2

alcohol [ăl′kə höl′] **39** 22

alligator [ăl′ə gā′tər] **65** 8

almond(s) [ö′mənd(z)] **9** 31

Alps [ălps] **70** 44

Amazon River [ă′mə zŏn rĭv′ər]
    71 59

ambulance [ăm′byə ləns] **42** 6

amphibians [ăm fĭ′bē ənz] **65**

ammunition [ăm′yə nĭsh′ən] **48**

anchor [ăng′kər] **58** 24

Andes [ăn′dēz] **71** 43

ankle [ăng′kəl] **5** 49

animals [ăn′ə məlz] **62-69**

ant [ănt] **63** 12

Antarctic Ocean [ănt ärk′tĭk ō′shən]
    70 14

Antarctica [ănt ärk′tĭ kə] **70** 7

anteater [ănt′ē′tər] **66** 5

antenna [ăn tĕn′ə] **51** 46, **62** 1b

antler [ănt′lər] **67** 35a

apartment house
    [ə pärt′mənt hows′] **45** 23

apex [ā′pĕks] **79** 21

Appalachian Mountains
    [ăp′ə lā′chē ən mown′tənz] **71** 41

apple [ă′pəl] **8** 2

apricot [ăp′rə kŏt′] **9** 25

apron [ā′prən] **16** 6

aquatic mammals
    [ə kwŏ′tĭk mă′məlz] **68**

Arabian Sea [ə rā′bē ən sē′] **70** 30

arc [ärk] **79** 16

architect [är′kə tĕkt′] **86** 8

Arctic [ärk′tĭk] **70** 8

Arizona [ăr′ə zō′nə] **72** 3

Arkansas [är′kən sö′] **72** 4

arm [ärm] **4** 6, **100** 20

armadillo [är′mə dĭl′ō] **66** 2

armed forces [ärmd′för′səz] **48**

armpit [ärm′pĭt′] **4** 10

armrest [ärm′rĕst′] **50** 3

Army [är′mē] **48** 15

around [ə rownd′] **103** 2

artery [är′tə rē] **5** 69

artichoke [är′tə chōk′] **6** 11

artist [är′təst] **86** 3

arts [ärts] **86**

ashtray [ăsh′trā′] **16** 29

Asia [ā′zhə] **70** 5

asparagus [ə spăr′ə gəs] **6** 18

asteroid [ăs′tə royd′] **74** 20

astronaut [ăs′trə nŏt′] **75** 5

at [ăt] **102** 1

Atacama Desert
    [ăt′ə kŏ′mə dĕz′ərt] **71** 50

athletic supporter
    [ăth lĕ′tĭk sə pör′tər] **22** 4

atlas [ăt′ləs] **47** 20

attachments [ə tăch′mənts] **35** 17

attendant [ə tĕn′dənt] **39** 8, **53** 12

audience [ö′dē əns] **99** 15

audio [ö′dē ō′] **100**

aunt [ănt] **3** 6

Australia [ö strāl′yə] **70** 6

author [ö′thər] **47** 8

automatic transmission
    [ö′tə măt′ĭk trănz mĭ′shən] **50**

avocado [ăv′ə kŏ′dō] **9** 33

away from [ə wā′frŭm] **103** 5

axe [ăks] **42** 14

baboon [bă boon′] **69** 19

baby [bā′bē] **2** 5

baby carriage [bā′bē kăr′ĭj] **45** 27

baby lotion [bā′bē lō′shən] **33** 6

baby powder [bā′bē pow′dər] **33** 7

baby wipes [bā′bē wīps′] **33** 8

baby's room [bā′bēz room′] **33**

back [băk] **4** 11, **23** 19

backache [băk′āk′] **40** 8

backboard [băk′börd′] **92** 19

backhoe [băk′hō′] **82** 26

backpack [băk′păk′] **19** 4

backseat [băk′sēt′] **50** 32

backyard [băk′yärd′] **27**

back-up light [băk′əp līt′] **50** 30

bacon [bā′kən] **10** 11, **18,** 33

badge [băj] **43** 5

Baffin Bay [băf′ən bā′] **70** 16

bag [băg] **12** 8, **15** 25, **21** 35

baggage [băg′ĭj] **56** 8

bake [bāk] **31** 14

baked beans [bākt′bēnz′] **18** 3

baked goods [bākt goodz′] **14** 11

baked potato [bākt′pə tā′tō] **18** 20

baker [bā′kər] **84** 8

bakery [bā′kə rē] **44** 6

balance beam [băl′əns bēm′] **94** 24

balcony [băl′kə nē] **99** 14

(bale of) hay [bāl′əv hā′] **81** 13

ball [böl] **5** 52

ballet [bă lā′] **99**

ballfields [böl′fēldz′] **93**

ballpoint pen [böl′poynt pĕn′] **76** 22

Baltic Sea [böl′tĭk sē′] **70** 22

bananas [bə nă′nəz] **9** 20

Band-Aid [bănd′ād′] **39** 4

band shell [bănd′shĕl′] **87** 2

bandage [băn′dĭj] **39** 24

banister [băn′ə stər] **28** 11

banjo [băn′jō′] **98** 5

banking [băng′kĭng] **86**

bar [bär] **13** 18, **16** 24

bar stool [bär′stool′] **16** 25

barber [bär′bər] **84** 3

Barents Sea [băr′ənts sē′] **70** 23

barge [bärj] **58** 12

bark [bärk] **61** 35c

barn [bärn] **81** 5

barnyard [bärn′yärd′] **81** 8

barrel [băr′əl] **48** 23

barricade [băr′ə kād′] **82** 21

bartender [bär′tĕn′dər] **16** 21

base [bās] **79** 7, **93** 6

baseball [bās′böl′] **92**

baseball diamond [bās′böl dī′mənd]
93

baseline [bās′līn′] **95** 4

basin [bā′sən] **39** 16

basket [băs′kət] **92** 20

basketball [băs′kət böl′] **92, 92** 21

bass [bās] **98** 10

bass guitarist [bās′gə tär′əst] **99** 23

bassoon [bă soon′] **98** 14

bat [băt] **66** 4, **92** 5

batboy [băt′boy′] **93** 18

bath mat [băth′ măt′] **34** 12

bath towel [băth′ tow′əl] **34** 24

bathing suit [bā′dhĭng soot′] **90** 18

bathing trunks [bā′ dhĭng trŭngks′]
91 33

bathrobe [băth′ rōb] **22** 20

bathroom [băth′ room′] **34**

bathtub [băth′ tŭb′] **34** 11

baton [bə tŏn′] **99** 9

batter [băt′ ər] **92** 7, **93** 14

battery [băt′ə rē] **51** 54

batting helmet [băt′ĭng hĕl′mət] **92** 6

battleship [băt′əl shĭp′] **48** 5

Bay of Bengal [bā′ əv bĕn göl′] **70** 32

bayonet [bā′ ə nĕt′] **48** 24

bays [bāz] **70**

beach [bēch] **90**

beach ball [bēch′ böl′] **90** 11

beach chair [bēch′ chër′] **90** 20

beach towel [bēch′ tow′ əl] **90** 15

beach umbrella [bēch′əm brĕl′ə]
90 21

beads [bēdz] **23** 7

beak [bēk] **64** 3a

beaker [bē′ kər] **78** 23

beard [bïrd] **4** 39

bears [bërz] **69**

beat [bēt] **31** 8

Beaufort Sea [bō′ fərt sē′] **70** 15

beaver [bē′vər] **66** 12

bed [bĕd] **32** 21

bed rest [bĕd′ rĕst′] **41** 1

bedroom [bĕd′room′] **32**

bedspread [bĕd′sprĕd′] **32** 23

bee [bē] **63** 19

beef [bēf] **10** 1

beef stew [bēf′ stoo′] **18** 14

beer [bïr] **16** 23

beet(s) [bēts] **7** 33

beetle [bē′təl] **63** 10

behind [bə hīnd′] **102** 9

below [bə lō′] **102** 3

belt [bĕlt] **20** 16

bench [bĕnch] **43** 16, **44** 14, **78** 24,
87 10

beret [bə rā′] **19** 22

Bering Sea [bër′ĭng sē′] **70** 34

berries [bër′ēz] **8**

between [bə twēn′] **102** 4

beverages [bĕv′rə jəz] **14** 14

bib [bĭb] **33** 20

bicycle [bī′sĭ kəl] **52** 15

big [bĭg] **24** 8

(Big Dipper) constellation
[bĭg′dĭ′pər kŏn stə lā′shən] **74** 3

big toe [bĭg′ tō′] **5** 53

bike stand [bīk′ stănd′] **52** 14

biker [bī′kər] **90** 4

bikes [bīks] **52**

(bikini) panties [bə kē′ nē păn′ tēz]
22 11

bill [bĭl] **64** 24a

bin [bĭn] **15** 16

binding [bīn′ dĭng] **95** 16

binoculars [bə nŏk′ yə lərs] **90** 7

birch [bürch] **61** 32

birds [bürdz] **64**

biscuit [bĭs′ kət] **18** 27

bison [bī′ sən] **67** 19

bit [bĭt] **37** 43a

black bear [blăk′ bër′] **69** 21

black bean(s) [blăk′ bēn(z)′] **6** 14

black eye [blăk′ ī′] **40** 5

Black Sea [blăk′ sē′] **70** 26

blackberries [blăk′ bër′ ēz] **8** 12

bladder [blă′ dər] **5** 72

blade [blād] **94** 27

blanket [blăng′ket] **32** 20

blazer [blā′zer] **20** 2

bleach [blēch] **35** 26

blender [blĕn′dər] **30** 12

blimp [blĭmp] **57** 5

blinds [blīndz] **32** 12

block [blŏk] **33** 32

blouse [blows] **21** 34

blue jay [bloo′ ja′] **64** 8

(blue) jeans [bloo′ jēnz′] **19** 6

blueberries [bloo′ bër′ēz] **8** 14

blueprints [bloo′ prĭnts′] **82** 6

blush [blŭsh] **23** 32

board [börd] **82** 16

boarding [bör′ dĭng] **56**

boarding pass [bör′ dĭng păs′] **56** 18

boardwalk [börd′ wök′] **90** 1

body [bŏ′ dē] **4**

boil [boyl] **31** 16

bollard [bŏl′ ərd] **58** 26

bolt [bōlt] **37** 38

bomb [bŏm] **48** 3

bomber [bŏm′ ər] **48** 2

bongos [bŏng′ gōz] **98** 22

book [book] **13** 17

(book of) matches [book′ əv mă′ chəz]
16 28

bookcase [book′ kās] **28** 22, **83** 20

bookstore [book′ stör] **45** 18

boom [boom] **59** 7

booth [booth] **16** 9

boots [boots] **19** 21, **21** 32

bottle [bŏt′ əl] **12** 3, **33** 17

bottle opener [bŏt′ əl ō′ pə nər] **30** 6

bounce [bowns] **97** 11

bow [bō] **98** 7a

bow [bow] **58** 5

bowl [bōl] **13** 23

bowling [bōl′ ĭng] **94**

bowling ball [bōl/ĭng böl/] **94** 6

box [bŏks] **13** 12

box seat [bŏks/ sēt/] **99** 11

box spring [bŏks/ sprĭng/] **32** 18

boxer shorts [bŏk/ sər shörts/] **22** 2

boxing [bŏk/ sĭng] **94**

boy's frame [boyz/ frām/] **52** 11

bra(ssiere) [brŏ]/[brə zïr/] **22** 13

brace [brās] **36** 9

bracelet [brās/ lət] **23** 9

brain [brān] **5** 57

brake [brāk] **50** 26, **52** 17

brake light [brāk/ līt/] **50** 29

branch [brănch] **61** 35a

brass [brăs] **98**

bread [brĕd] **14** 12

bread and butter plate
  [brĕd/ ənd bŭt/ ər plāt/] **29** 11

break [brāk] **31** 7

breast [brĕst] **11** 21

bricks [brĭks] **82** 12

bridle path [brīd/ əl păth/] **87** 7

briefcase [brēf/ kās/] **21** 37

briefs [brēfs] **22** 12

broccoli [brŏk/ ə lē] **6** 2

broil [broyl] **31** 13

broiler [broy/ lər] **30** 33

broken bone [brō/ kən bōn/] **40** 15

broom [brōōm] **35** 7

brother [brŭdh/ ər] **3** 9

brother-in-law [brŭdh/ ər ən lö/] **3** 11

bruise [brōōz] **40** 17

brush [brŭsh] **76** 18

brussels sprouts [brŭs/ əl sprowts/] **6** 4

bucket [bŭk/ ət] **35** 15

bucket seat [bŭk/ ət sēt/] **50** 16

buckle [bŭk/ əl] **20** 17

bud [bŭd] **60** 18a

buffet [bə fā/] **29** 29

builder [bĭl/ dər] **82** 5

building number [bĭl/ dĭng nŭm/ bər]
  45 24

bulb [bŭlb] **60** 8a

bull [bŏŏl] **67** 34

bulldozer [bŏŏl/ dō/ zər] **82** 27

bullet [bŏŏl/ ĭt] **48** 26

bulletin board [bŏŏl/ ĭ tən börd/] **76** 7

bumper [bŭm/ pər] **33** 5

bun [bŭn] **18** 7

bunch [bŭnch] **8** 1

Bunsen burner [bŭn/ sən bür/ nər]
  78 20

buoy [bōō/ ē]/[boy] **58** 16

bureau [byŏŏr/ ō] **32** 9

burn [bürn] **17** 14, **40** 18

burner [bür/ nər] **30** 29

bus [bŭs] **53** 20, **54**

bus driver [bŭs/ drī/ vər] **54** 3

bus stop [bŭs/ stŏp/] **44** 13

busboy [bŭs/ boy/] **16** 3

bushes [bŏŏsh/ əz] **61** 41

business workers [bĭz/ nəs wür/ kərz] **86**

butcher [bŏŏ/ chər] **84** 13

butter [bŭt/ ər] **18** 18

buttercup [bŭt/ ər kŭp/] **60** 17

butterfly [bŭt/ ər flī/] **63** 3

buttocks [bŭt/ əks] **4** 15

button [bŭt/ ən] **20** 3, **101** 9

buttonhole [bŭt/ ən hōl/] **101** 8

C-clamp [sē/ klămp/] **36** 2

cab driver [kăb/ drī/ vər] **55** 26

cabbage [kăb/ ĭj] **6** 3

cabin [kăb/ ĭn] **56** 19

cabin cruiser [kăb/ ĭn krōō/ zər] **59** 16

cabinet [kăb/ ə nət] **30** 22

cable [kā/ bəl] **52** 23

cable car [kā/ bəl kär/] **55** 32

cactus [kăk/ təs] **61** 40

calculator [kăl/ kyə lā/ tər] **83** 19,
  100 34

calendar [kăl/ ən dər] **83** 9

calf [kăf] **4** 20, **67** 31

California [kăl/ ə för/ nyə] **72** 5

call card [köl/ kärd/] **47** 6

call number [köl/ nŭm/ bər] **47** 7

call slip [köl/ slĭp/] **47** 12

camel [kăm/ əl] **67** 33

camera [kăm/ ər ə] **100** 8

cameraperson [kăm/ ər ə pür/ sən] **86** 10

camisole [kăm/ ə sōl/] **22** 9

camp stove [kămp/ stōv/] **89** 25

camper [kăm/ pər] **53** 16

campfire [kămp/ fīr/] **89** 31

camping [kăm/ pĭng] **89**

can [kăn] **12** 10

can opener [kăn/ ō/ pə nər] **30** 4

canary [kə nër/ ē] **64** 14

candle [kăn/ dəl] **29** 27

candlestick [kăn/ dəl stĭk/] **29** 28

canister [kăn/ ə stər] **30** 15

canned goods [kănd/ gŏŏdz/] **14** 13

cannon [kăn/ ən] **48** 11

canoe [kə nōō/] **59** 2

cantaloupe [kăn/ tə lōp/] **9** 36

canyon [kăn/ yən] **88** 3

cap [kăp] **19** 2, **21** 43, **92** 11

capsule [kăp/ səl] **41** 5

car [kär] **54** 9

card catalog [kärd/ kăt/ ə lög] **47** 4

cardigan [kär/ dĭ gən] **21** 26

cardinal [kärd/ nəl] **64** 11

cargo [kär/ gō] **58** 10

cargo area [kär/ gō ër/ ē ə] **57** 12

cargo bay [kär/ gō bā/] **75** 9

cargo door [kär/ gō dör/] **57** 13

Caribbean Sea [kăr/ ə bē/ ən sē /]
  70 20

carpenter [kär/ pən tər] **85** 2

carpenter's rule [kär/ pən tərz rōōl/]
  36 1

carrot(s) [kăr/ ət(s)] **7** 32

carry [kăr/ ē] **26** 16

carry-on bag [kăr/ ē ŏn băg/] **56** 2

cars [kärz] **50-51**

carton [kär/ tən] **12** 1

cartridge needle [kär/ trĭj nē/ dəl]
  100 19

carve [kärv] **31** 6

cash register [kăsh/ rĕ/ jə stər] **15** 21

cashew(s) [kăsh/ ōō(z)] **9** 27

cashier [kă shïr/] **15** 22

Caspian Sea [kăs/ pē ən sē/] **70** 27

casserole dish [kăs/ ə rōl dĭsh/] **30** 14

cassette [kə sĕt/] **100** 26

cassette deck [kə sĕt/ dĕk/] **100** 22

cast [kăst] **39** 5

cat [kăt] **68** 4

catch [kăch] **96** 4

catcher [kăch/ ər] **92** 2, **93** 16

catcher's mask [kăch/ ərz măsk/] **92** 3

catcher's mitt [kăch/ ərz mĭt/] **92** 4

caterpillar [kăt/ ər pĭl/ ər] **63** 1

cattle [kăt/ əl] **81** 20

Caucasus [kö/ kə səs] **71** 45

cauliflower [kŏl′ ə flow′ ər] **6** 1

ceiling [sē′ lĭng] **28** 2

ceiling fan [sē′ lĭng făn′] **28** 1

celery [sĕl′ ə rē] **6** 10

cello [chĕl′ o] **98** 9

cement [sə mĕnt′] **82** 10

cement mixer [sə mĕnt′ mĭk′ sər] **82** 25

cement truck [sə mĕnt′ trŭk′] **49** 13

center [sĕn′ tər] **79** 13, **93** 27

center divider [sĕn′ tər də vī′ dər] **53** 18, **82** 24

center fielder [sĕn′ tər fēl′ dər] **93** 2

center lane [sĕn′ tər lān′] **53** 6

centerboard [sĕn′ tər börd′] **59** 6

centipede [sĕn′ tə pēd′] **63** 22

chain [chān] **23** 5, **52** 18

chair [chër] **29** 17

chalk [chök] **76** 10

chalk tray [chök′ trā′] **76** 9

chalkboard [chök′ börd′] **76** 5

chandelier [shăn′ də lïr′] **29** 3

change (the sheets) [chānj′ dhə shēts′] **38** 13

changing table [chān′ jĭng tā′ bəl] **33** 9

charcoal briquettes [chär′ kōl brĭ kĕts′] **27** 23

chart [chärt] **39** 10

check [chĕk] **15** 27, **16** 14

checked [chĕkt] **24** 18

checkout counter [chĕk′ owt kown′ tər] **15** 26

checkout desk [chĕk′ owt dĕsk′] **47** 2

cheerleaders [chïr′ lē′ dərz] **93** 20

cheek [chēk] **4** 35

cherries [chër′ ēz] **9** 19

cherry picker [chër′ ē pĭk′ ər] **82** 18

chest [chĕst] **4** 12

chest of drawers [chĕst′ əv drörz′] **32** 30

chestnut(s) [chĕs′ nŭt(s)] **9** 32

chick [chĭk] **64** 22

chicken [chĭk′ ən] **11** 24, **64** 23

child's seat [chīldz′ sēt′] **50** 33

children [chĭl′ drən] **2** 7

chills [chĭlz] **40** 4

chimney [chĭm′ nē] **27** 9

chimpanzee [chĭm păn′ zē] **69** 16

chin [chĭn] **4** 3

china [chī′ nə] **29** 1

china closet [chī′ nə klöz′ ət] **29** 2

chipmunk [chĭp′ mŭnk] **66** 6

chop [chŏp] **26** 11, **31** 11

chops [chŏps] **10** 9, **10** 15

chorus [kör′ əs] **99** 18

(chrysanthe)mum [krə săn′ thə məm]/[mŭm] **60** 4

cigarette [sĭg′ ə rĕt′] **16** 31

circle [sür′ kəl] **79** 11

circuit breaker [sür′ kət brā′ kər] **35** 5

circular saw [sür′ kyə lər sö′] **36** 20

circumference [sür kŭm′ fə rəns] **79** 17

citrus fruits [sĭ′ trəs frōōts′] **8**

city [sĭt′ ē] **44-45**

clam(s) [klăm(z)] **11** 32

clamp [klămp] **78** 7

clarinet [klăr′ ə nĕt′] **98** 16

clasp [klăsp] **23** 17

classroom [klăs′ rōōm′] **76**

claw [klö] **62** 13a, **68** 2a

clean [klēn] **24** 6, **26** 2

cleanser [klĕn′ zər] **35** 9

clear [klïr] **17** 6

cliff [klĭf] **89** 21

clip-on earring [klĭp′ ŏn ïr′ ĭng] **23** 15

clock [klŏk] **76** 2

close (v) [klōz] **77** 5

closed [klōzd] **24** 16

closet [klŏz′ ət] **32** 3

cloth diaper [klöth′ dī′ pər] **33** 13

clothes [klōz] **19-24**

clothesline [klōz′ līn′] **35** 19

clothespins [klōz′ pĭnz′] **35** 20

cloudy [klow′ dē] **25** 2

clove [klōv] **7** 25a

cloverleaf [klō′ vər lēf′] **53** 4

clubs [klŭbz] **95** 5

clutch [klŭch] **50** 25

coach [kōch] **93** 21

coal [kōl] **80** 7

coal mine [kōl′ mīn′] **80** 6

coaster [kō′ stər] **16** 27

coat [kōt] **19** 24, **42** 13

cob [kŏb] **6** 12a

cobra [kō′ brə] **65** 11

cockpit [kŏk′ pĭt′] **56** 13

cockroach [kŏk′ rōch′] **63** 9

cocktail lounge [kŏk′ tāl lownj′] **16**

cocktail waitress [kŏk′ tāl wā′ trəs] **16** 32

cocoon [kə kōōn′] **63** 2

coconut [kō′ kə nŭt′] **8** 3

coffee [kö′ fē] **18** 35

coffeemaker [kö′ fē mā′ kər] **30** 31

coffeepot [kö′ fē pŏt′] **29** 18

coffee table [kö′ fē tā′ bəl] **28** 26

coins [koynz] **13** 26

colander [kŏl′ ən dər] **30** 7

cold [kōld] **25** 10, **40** 11

cold water faucet [kōld′ wŏ tər fö′ sət] **34** 18

collar [kŏl′ ər] **20** 20

colonial-style house [kə lō′ nē əl stīl hows′] **27**

Colorado [kŏl′ ə rŏd′ ō] **72** 6

column [kŏl′ əm] **50** 13

comb [kōm] **32** 6

combine (n) [kŏm′ bīn] **81** 17

comet [kŏm′ ət] **74** 2

comforter [kŭm′ fər tər] **32** 22

command module [kə mănd′ mŏj′ ōol] **75** 8

communication satellite [kə myōō′ nə kā shən săt′ ə līt] **75** 2

commuter [kə myōō′ tər] **55** 17

commuter train [kə myōō′ tər trān′] **55** 14

compact disc (CD) [kŏm′ păkt dĭsk′]/[sē′ dē′] **100** 27

compact disc player [kŏm′ păkt dĭsk′ plā′ ər] **100** 28

computer [kəm pyōō′ tər] **76** 8, **83** 16, **100**

computer programmer [kəm pyōō′ tər prō′ grăm ər] **86** 16

conductor [kən dŭk′ tər] **54** 7, **99** 8

cone [kōn] **61** 34b, **79** 28, **82** 19

conga [kŏng′ gə] **98** 20

Congo River [kŏng′ gō rĭv′ ər] **71** 62

Connecticut [kə nĕ′ tĭ kət] **72** 7

constellation [kŏn′ stə lā′ shən] **74** 3

construction [kən strŭk′ shən] **82**

(construction) boots [kən strŭk′ shən bōōts′] **21** 32

索引

construction site [kən strŭk′ shən sīt′] **82**

construction worker
 [kən strŭk′ shən wür′ kər] **82** 14

container [kən tā′nər] **12** 2, **58** 7

(container)ship [kən tā′ nər shĭp′] **58** 9

containers [kən tā′ nərz] **12**

continents [kŏn′ tə nənts] **70**

control tower [kən trōl′ tow′ər] **57** 20

conveyor belt [kən vā′ər bĕlt] **15** 23,
 56 12

cook (n) [kook] **16** 1

cook (v) [kook] **17** 4

cookie [kook′ ē] **18** 22

cool [kool] **25** 9

cooler [koo′ lər] **91** 41

cooling tower [koo′lĭng tow′ər] **80** 16

copilot [kō′pī lət] **56** 16

cord [körd] **32** 26a, **54** 1

(corduroy) pants [kör′ də roy pănts′]
 21 27

core [kör] **8** 2b, **80** 14

cork [körk] **16** 18

corkscrew [körk′ skroo′] **16** 17

corn [körn] **6** 12, **60** 24

corner [kör′ nər] **44** 3

corral [kə răl′] **81** 24

cosmetics [kŏz mĕt′ ĭks] **23**

cotton balls [kŏt′ ən bölz′] **39** 23

cotton swab [kŏt′ ən swŏb′] **33** 10

counter [kown′ tər] **30** 27

court [kört] **43**, **94** 13

court officer [kört′ ö′ fə sər] **43** 19

court reporter [kört′ rə pör′ tər] **43** 14

cousin [kŭz′ən] **3** 7

cow [kow] **67** 32

cowboy [kow′ boy′] **81** 21

cowgirl [kow′ gürl′] **81** 22

crab(s) [kră b(z)] **11** 36, **62** 9

cradle [krā′ dəl] **33** 26

cranberries [krăn′ bër′ ēz] **8** 13

crane [krān] **58** 6

creamer [krē′ mər] **29** 24

crew [kroo] **75** 12

(crewneck) sweater
 [kroo′ nĕk swĕt′ ər] **19** 7

crib [krĭb] **33** 4

criket [krĭk′ ət] **63** 5

crime [krīm] **43**

crochet [krō shā′] **101** 28

crochet hook [krō′ shā′ hook′] **101** 29

crocus [krō′ kəs] **60** 9

cross-country skiing
 [krös′ kŭn trē skē′ ĭng] **94**

crosswalk [krös′ wök′] **44** 4

crow [krō] **64** 3

crutch [krŭch] **39** 7

cube [kyoob] **79** 27

cubicle [kyoo′ bə kəl] **83** 5

cucumber(s) [kyoo′ kŭm bər(z)] **7** 20

cuff links [kŭf′ lĭnks′] **23** 12

cup [kŭp] **13** 19, **29** 20

curb [kürb] **45** 26

curtain [kür′ tən] **32** 10, **99** 1

curtain rings [kür′ tən rĭngz′] **34** 2

curtain rod [kür′ tən rŏd′] **34** 1

curve [kürv] **79** 3

cushion [koosh′ ən] **28** 24

customer [kŭs′ tə mər] **15** 17

cut (v) [kŭt] **31** 9

cut (n) [kŭt] **40** 16

cutting board [kŭt′ ĭng börd′] **30** 26

cylinder [sĭl′ ĭn dər] **79** 26

cymbals [sĭm′ bəlz] **98** 18

daffodil [dăf′ ə dĭl] **60** 8

dairy cow [dër′ ē kow′] **81** 11

dairy farm [dër′ ē färm′] **81**

dairy products [dër′ ē prŏd′ ŭkts] **14** 4

daisy [dā′ zē] **60** 5

dam [dăm] **80** 18

dance [dăns] **99**

dancer [dăn′ sər] **99** 3

dark [därk] **24** 10

dashboard [dăsh′ börd′] **50** 19

date [dāt] **9** 23

daughter [dö′ tər] **3** 15

deck [dĕk] **27** 5, **58** 22

deer [dïr] **67** 26

defendant [də fĕn′ dənt] **43** 23

defense attorney [də fĕns′ ə tür′ nē]
 43 22

Delaware [dĕl′ ə wär′] **72** 8

deli counter [dĕl′ ē kown′ tər] **14** 1

delivery boy [də lĭv′ ə rē boy′] **85** 10

delivery person [də lĭv′ ə rē pür′ sən]
 49 10

dental care [dĕn′ təl kër′] **39**

dentist [dĕn′ tĭst] **39** 17

department store [də pärt′ mənt stör′]
 44 5

depth [dĕpth] **79** 33

derrick [dĕr′ ĭk] **80** 2

deserts [dĕz′ ərts] **71**

desk [dĕsk] **28** 14, **76** 16, **83** 13

detective [də tĕk′ tĭv] **43** 2

diagonal [dī ăg′ ə nəl] **79** 20

diameter [dī ăm′ ə tər] **79** 12

dictionary [dĭk′ shə nër′ ē] **47** 24

diesel fuel [dē′ zəl fyoo′ əl] **80** 34

dig [dĭg] **26** 3

dime [dīm] **13** 29

dinghy [dĭng′ ē] **59** 18

dining room [dī′ nĭng room′] **29**

dipstick [dĭp′ stĭk′] **51** 58

dirt bike [dürt′ bīk′] **52** 8

dirty [dür′ tē] **24** 5

disc jockey (DJ) [dĭsk′ jŏk′ ē]/[dē′ jā]
 86 9

dish drainer [dĭsh′ drā′ nər] **30** 2

dish towel [dĭsh′ tow′ əl] **30** 18

dishwasher [dĭsh′ wŏsh′ ər] **30** 1

dishwashing liquid
 [dĭsh′ wŏsh ĭng lĭ′ kwĭd] **30** 10

disposable diaper
 [dīs pō′ zə bəl dī′ pər] **33** 12

dissection kit [dĭ sĕk′ shən kĭt′] **78** 33

dive [dīv] **97** 14

dock [dŏk] **58** 28

doctor [dŏk′ tər] **39** 11

dogs [dögz] **69**

dogwood [dög′ wood′] **61** 28

doll [dŏl] **33** 28

doll house [dŏl′ hows′] **33** 25

dollar bills [dŏl′ ər bĭlz′] **13** 25

dolly [dŏl′ ē] **56** 6

dolphin [dŏl′ fĭn] **68** 13

donkey [dŏng′ kē] **67** 23

door handle [dör′ hăn′ dəl] **50** 4

door lock [dör′ lŏk′] **50** 1

doorman [dör′ mən] **85** 11

down [down] **103** 3

down vest [down′ vĕst′] **19** 12

dragonfly [drăg′ ən flī′] **63** 4

drain [drān] **34** 9

drainpipe [drān′ pīp′] **27** 18

drapes [drāps] **28** 23

draw [drö] **77** 11

drawer [drör] **47** 5

dress [drĕs] **20** 22

dried fruits [drīd/ frōots/] **9**

drill [drĭl] **39** 15

drink [drĭngk] **17** 2

drive [drīv] **97** 15

driveway [drīv/ wā/] **27** 1

drugstore [drŭg/ stör/] **45** 22

drum [drŭm] **98** 19

drummer [drŭm/ ər] **99** 27

drumsticks [drŭm/ stĭks/] **98** 19a

dry [drī] **25** 14, **38** 9

dryer [drī/ər] **35** 24

duck [dŭk] **11** 25, **64** 25

(duck) pond [dŭk/ pŏnd/] **87** 8

dugout [dŭg/ owt/] **93** 13

dump truck [dŭmp/ trŭk/] **49** 14

dust [dŭst] **38** 15

dustpan [dŭst/ păn/] **35** 8

eagle [ē/ gəl] **64** 5

ear [ïr] **4** 34

(ear of) corn [ïr/ əv körn/] **6** 12

earmuffs [ïr/ mŭfs/] **19** 10

earrings [ïr/ ĭngz]' **23** 1

Earth [ürth] **74** 8, **13**

east [ēst] **71** 73

East China Sea [ēst/ chī/ nə sē/] **70** 38

eat [ēt] **17** 1

eel [ēl] **65** 4

egg [ĕg] **18** 32, **64** 13

egg roll [ĕg/ rōl/] **18** 25

eggplant [ĕg/ plănt/] **7** 21

elbow [ĕl/ bō] **4** 8

electric drill [ĭ lĕk/ trĭk drĭl/] **37** 43

electric guitar [ĭ lĕk/ trĭk gĭ tär/] **99** 26

electric generator [ĭ lĕk/ trĭk gĕn/ ə rā tər] **80** 21

electrical tape [ĭ lĕk/ trĭ kəl tāp/] **37** 34

electrician [ĭ lĕk trĭ/ shən] **85** 6

electricity [ĭ lĕk trĭs/ ĭ tē] **80** 32

electronics [ĭ lĕk trŏn/ ĭks] **100**

elephant [ĕl/ ə fənt] **66** 17

elevator [ĕl/ ə vā/ tər] **45** 17, **80** 9

elm [ĕlm] **61** 36

embroidery [ĕm broi/ də rē] **101** 27

cmergency brake [ĭ mür/ jən sē brāk/] **50** 15

emery board [ĕm/ ə rē börd/] **23** 24

encyclopedia [ĕn sī/ klə pē/ dē ə] **47** 25

end table [ĕnd/ tā/ bəl] **28** 29

end zone [ĕnd/ zōn/] **93** 23

energy [ĕn/ ər jē] **80**

engagement ring [ĕn gāj/ mənt rĭng/] **23** 3

engine [ĕn/ jən] **51, 52** 32

engineer [ĕn/ jə nïr/] **55** 15

enter [ĕn/ tər] **77** 14

entrance ramp [ĕn/ trəns rămp/] **53** 21

envelope [ĕn/ və lōp/] **46** 16, **83** 31

equator [ĭ kwā/ tər] **71** 70

erase [ĭ rās/] **77** 3

eraser [ĭ rā/ sər] **76** 11

escarole [ĕs/ kə rōl/] **6** 7

esophagus [ĭ sŏf/ ə gəs] **5** 61

eucalyptus [yōō/ kə lĭp/ təs] **61** 27

Europe [yŏŏr/ əp] **70** 3

examining table [ĭg zăm/ ə nĭng tā/ bəl] **39** 6

exhaust pipe [ĭg zöst/ pīp/] **52** 33

exit ramp [ĕg/ zĭt rămp/] **53** 2

exit sign [ĕg/ zĭt sīn/] **53** 24

Express Mail (package) [ĭk sprĕs/ māl păk/ ĭj] **46** 23

extension cord [ĭk stĕn/ shən körd/] **36** 5

eye [ī] **5**

eye drops [ī/ drŏps/] **41** 10

eye shadow [ī/ shă/ dō] **23** 30

eyebrow [ī/ brow/] **5** 44

eyebrow pencil [ī/ brow pĕn/ səl] **23** 26

eyelashes [ī/ lăsh/ əz] **5** 46

eyelid [ī/ lĭd/] **5** 45

eyeliner [ī/ lī/ nər] **23** 33

fabric softener [făb/ rĭk sö/ fə nər] **35** 27

face [fās] **4** 1

face guard [fās/ gärd/] **92** 15

factory work [făk/ tə rē würk/] **85**

fairway [fĕr/ wā/] **95** 12

fall [föl] **96** 7

Fall [föl] **26**

family [făm/ ə lē] **3**

family restaurant [făm/ ə lē rĕs/ tər ənt] **16**

fan belt [făn/ bĕlt/] **51** 53

fare [fĕr] **55** 21

fare box [fĕr/ bŏks/] **54** 5

farmhouse [färm/ hows/] **81** 3

farmer [fär/ mər] **81** 7

farming [fär/ mĭng] **81**

fashion designer [făsh/ ən də zī/ nər] **86** 6

father [fŏdh/ ər] **3** 5

faucet [fö/ sĭt] **34** 17, 18

fawn [fön] **67** 27

feather [fĕdh/ər] **64** 7a

feather duster [fĕdh/ ər dŭs/ tər] **35** 2

fence [fĕns] **81** 9

fender [fĕn/ dər] **52** 10

ferry [fĕr/ ē] **58** 17

fever [fē/ vər] **40** 2

field [fēld] **81** 16

fields and courses [fēldz/ ənd kör/ səz] **95**

fig [fĭg] **9** 21

fighter plane [fī/ tər plān/] **48** 1

file cabinet [fīl/ kăb/ ə nət] **83** 21

file clerk [fīl/ klürk/] **83** 23

file folder [fīl/ fōl/ dər] **83** 22

filet [fĭ lā/] **11** 28

fill [fĭl] **26** 9

film [fĭlm] **100** 10, **100** 17

filter paper [fĭl/ tər pā/ pər] **78** 16

fin [fĭn] **65** 3b

finger [fĭng/ gəɪ] **4** 25

fingernail [fĭng/ gər nāl/] **4** 23

fingerprints [fĭng/ gər prĭnts/] **43** 24

finish line [fĭn/ ĭsh līn/] **95** 21

fire [fīr] **28** 9, **42** 5

fire engine [fīr/ ĕn/ jən] **42** 2

fire escape [fīr/ ə skāp/] **42** 4

fire extinguisher [fīr/ ĭk stĭng/ gwĭ shər] **42** 11

fire fighter [fīr/ fī/ tər] **42** 10

fire hydrant [fīr/ hī/ drənt] **42** 9

fire truck [fīr/ trŭk/] **42** 3

firefighting [fīr/ fī/ tĭng] **42**

firefly [fīr/ flī/] **63** 17

fireplace [fīr′ plās′] **28** 8

first baseman [fürst′ bās′ mən] **93** 8

first quarter [fürst′ kwör′ tər] **74** 23

fish [fĭsh] **11** 26, **65**

fisherman [fĭsh′ ər mən] **58** 2

fishing [fĭsh′ ĭng] **88**

fishing boat [fĭsh′ ĭng bōt′] **58** 1

fishing line [fĭsh′ ĭng līn′] **88** 8

fishing net [fĭsh′ ĭng nĕt′] **88** 9

fishing rod [fĭsh′ ĭng rŏd′] **88** 7

flag [flăg] **76** 1, **82** 20, **95** 9

flame [flām] **29** 26, **78** 21

flamingo [flə mĭng′ gō] **64** 29

flanker [flăng′ kər] **93** 31

flannel shirt [flăn′ əl shürt′] **19** 3

flare [flër] **51** 41

flash [flăsh] **100** 7

flashlight [flăsh′ līt′] **35** 3

flask [flăsk] **78** 2

(flat) sheet [flăt′ shēt′] **32** 19

flatbed [flăt′ bĕd′] **49** 18

flight attendant [flīt′ ə tĕn′ dənt] **56** 20

flight deck [flīt′ dĕk′] **75** 10

flight engineer [flīt′ ĕn jə nïr′] **56** 17

flipper [flĭp′ ər] **68** 12a

flippers [flĭp′ ərz] **91** 36

floor [flör] **32** 29

Florida [flör′ ə də] **72** 9

florist [flör′ ĭst] **84** 11

flounder [flown′ dər] **65** 7

flowers [flow′ ərz] **60**

flute [flōōt] **99** 13

fly [flī] **63** 18

flying mammal [flī′ ĭng mă′ məlz] **66**

foal [fōl] **67** 22

foggy [fŏg′ ē] **25** 12

fold [fōld] **38** 1

food [fōōd] **6-18**

foot [fŏŏt] **5**

football [fŏŏt′ böl′] **92, 92** 13

football field [fŏŏt′ böl fēld′] **93**

forceps [för′ səps] **78** 28

forearm [för′ ärm′] **4** 9

forehead [för′ hĕd′] **4** 32

forelegs [för′ lĕgz′] **66** 3d

foreman [för′ mən] **85** 13

fork [förk] **29** 12

forklift [förk′ lĭft′] **58** 4

foul line [fowl′ līn′] **93** 9

foundation [fown dā′ shən] **82** 11

four-door hatchback [för′ dör hăch′ băk] **51**

fox [fŏks] **68** 6

fractions [frăk′ shənz] **79**

frame [frām] **28** 4

frame backpack [frām′ băk′ păk] **89** 28

freezer [frē′ zər] **14** 3, **30** 20

freezing [frē′ zĭng] **25** 11

french fries [frĕnch′ frīz′] **18** 28

French horn [frĕnch′ hörn′] **98** 26

fried chicken [frīd′ chĭk′ ən] **18** 29

Frisbee™ [frĭz′ bē] **90** 13

frog [frŏg] **65** 17

from [frŭm] **103** 10

front bumper [frŭnt′ bŭm′ pər] **51** 51

frozen foods [frō′ zən fōōdz′] **14** 2

fruit and vegetable market [frōōt′ ənd vĕj′ tə bəl mär′ kət] **45** 28

fruit tree [frōōt′ trē′] **81** 2

fruits [frōōts] **8**

fry [frī] **31** 15

frying pan [frī′ ĭng păn′] **30** 5

fuel truck [fyōō′ əl trŭk′] **49** 3

full moon [fŏŏl′ mōōn′] **74** 24

full slip [fŏŏl′ slĭp′] **22** 10

fullback [fŏŏl′ băk′] **93** 34

funnel [fŭn′ əl] **78** 17

fuselage [fyōō′ sə lŏj′] **57** 14

galaxy [găl′ək sē] **74** 1

Ganges River [găn′ jēz rĭv′ ər] **71** 67

gangway [găng′ wā′] **58** 20

garage [gə rŏj′] **27** 2

garbage can [gär′ bĭj kăn′] **35** 31

garbage truck [gär′ bĭj trŭk′] **49** 6

garden hose [gär′ dən hōs′] **27** 14

gardener [gärd′ nər] **85** 3

gardenia [gär dēn′ yə] **60** 14

garlic [gär′ lĭk] **7** 25

garment bag [gär′ mənt băg′] **56** 1

garter belt [gär′ tər bĕlt′] **22** 14

(garter) snake [gär′ tər snāk′] **65** 9

gas gauge [găs′ gāj′] **50** 9

gas pump [găs′ pŭmp′] **53** 14

gas tank [găs′ tăngk′] **50** 34

gas(oline) [găs′ ə lēn′] **80** 28

(gauze) bandage [göz′ băn′ dĭj] **39** 24

gauze pads [göz′ pădz′] **39** 25

gavel [găv′ əl] **43** 12

gear [gïr] **89** 27

gear changer [gïr′ chān′ jər] **52** 22

gearshift [gïr′ shĭft′] **50** 17

geometrical figures [jē′ ə mĕ′ trĭ kəl fĭg′ yərz] **79**

Georgia [jör′ jə] **72** 10

geyser [gī′ zər] **80** 5

gibbon [gĭb′ ən] **69** 15

gill [gĭl] **65** 3c

giraffe [jə răf′] **67** 29

girdle [gür′ dəl] **22** 15

girl [gürl] **2** 9

girl's frame [gürlz′ frām′] **52** 3

give [gĭv] **17** 9

glass [glăs] **12** 20

glasses [glăs′ əz] **21** 44

glider [glī′ dər] **57** 4

globe [glōb] **47** 19

glove [glŭv] **92** 12, **94** 11, **94** 15

glove compartment [glŭv′ kəm pärt′ mənt] **50** 20

gloves [glŭvz] **19** 1

glue [glōō] **37** 33, **76** 17

goal [gōl] **92** 25

goalie [gōl′ ē] **92** 24

goalpost [gōl′ pōst′] **93** 35

goat [gōt] **67** 28

Gobi Desert [gō′ bē dĕz′ ərt] **71** 54

golf [gŏlf] **94**

golf bag [gŏlf′ băg′] **95** 7

golf ball [gŏlf′ böl′] **94** 7

golf cart [gŏlf′ kärt′] **95** 8

golf course [gŏlf′ körs′] **95**

golfer [gŏl′ fər] **94** 10

goose [gōōs] **64** 26

gooseberries [gōōs′ bĕr′ ēz] **8** 11

gopher [gō′ fər] **66** 8

gorilla [gə rĭl′ ə] **69** 17

graduated cylinder [grăj′ ōō ā tĭd sĭl′ ən dər] **78** 25

grains [grānz] **60**

granddaughter [grănd′ dö′ tər] **2** 11

grandfather [grănd′ fŏ′ dhər] **3** 2

grandmother [grănd′ mŭ′ dhər] **3** 1

grandparents [grănd păr′ ənts] **2** 10

grandson [grănd′ sŭn′] **2** 12

grapefruit [grăp**/** frōōt**/**] **8** 7

grapes [grāps] **8** 1

graph paper [grăf**/** pā**/** pər] **78** 11

grass [grăs] **27** 15

grasses [grăs**/** əz] **60**

grasshopper [grăs**/** hŏp**/** ər] **63** 6

grate [grāt] **31** 2

Great Sandy Desert
[grāt**/** săn**/** dē dĕz**/** ərt] **71** 55

green [grēn] **95** 10

greengrocer [grēn**/** grō**/** sər] **84** 7

grill [grĭl] **27** 22, **88** 12

grizzly bear [grĭz**/** lē bër**/**] **69** 23

groceries [grō**/** sə rēz] **15** 24

ground beef [grownd**/** bēf**/**] **10** 2

grounding plug [grown**/** dĭng plŭg**/**]
36 7

guitar [gĭ tär**/**] **98** 11

Gulf of Alaska [gŭlf**/** əv ə lăs**/**kə]
70 17

Gulf of Guinea [gŭlf**/** əv gĭn**/** ē] **70** 25

Gulf of Mexico [gŭlf**/** əv mĕk sə kō]
70 19

gulfs [gŭlfs] **70**

gun [gŭn] **43** 7

gun turret [gŭn**/** tür**/** ət] **48** 12

gutter [gŭt**/** ər] **27** 10, **94** 3

gymnast [jĭm**/** nəst] **94** 23

gymnastics [jĭm năs**/** tĭks] **94**

hacksaw [hăk**/** sö**/**] **36** 18

hair [hër] **4** 30

hair dryer [hër**/** drī**/** ər] **34** 26

hairbrush [hër**/** brŭsh**/**] **32** 7

hairdresser [hër**/** drĕs**/** ər] **84** 10

half (1/2) [hăf] **79** 30

half slip [hăf**/** slĭp**/**] **22** 8

halfback [hăf**/** băk**/**] **93** 33

hall [höl] **76** 12

ham [hăm] **10** 12

hamburger [hăm**/**bür**/** gər] **18** 9

hammer [hăm**/** ər] **36** 13

hammock [hăm**/** ok] **27** 11

hamper [hăm**/** pər] **34** 28

hand [hănd] **4**

hand brake [hănd**/** brāk**/**] **52** 24

hand grenade [hănd**/** grə nād**/**] **48** 29

hand towel [hănd**/** tow**/** əl] **34** 23

hand truck [hănd**/** trŭk**/**] **87** 4

handball [hănd**/** böl**/**] **94, 94** 12

handcuffs [hănd**/** kŭfs**/**] **43** 4

handicrafts [hăn**/** dē krăfts**/**] **101**

handlebars [hăn**/** dəl bärz**/**] **52** 2

hang [hăng] **38** 6

hang glider [hăng**/** glī**/** dər] **57** 6

hangar [hăng**/** ər] **57** 17

hanger [hăng**/** ər] **32** 2

hard hat [härd**/** hăt**/**] **21** 28, **82** 4

harmonica [här mŏn**/** ə kə] **98** 30

harness [här**/** nəs] **89** 22

harp [härp] **98** 6

hat [hăt] **19** 18

hatchback [hăch**/** băk**/**] **51** 43

hatchet [hăch**/** ət] **36** 17

Hawaii [hə wŏ**/** ē] **72** 11

hawk [hök] **64** 7

hay [hā] **81** 13

hazelnut(s) [hā**/** zəl nŭt(s)**/**] **9** 30

head [hĕd] **4, 37** 42a

(head of) cauliflower
[hĕd**/** əv köl ə flow**/** ər] **6** 1

head protector [hĕd prə tĕk**/** tər] **94** 14

headache [hĕd**/** āk**/**] **40** 6

headboard [hĕd**/** börd**/**] **32** 14

headlights [hĕd**/** līts**/**] **51** 48

headphones [hĕd**/** fōnz**/**] **100** 29

headrest [hĕd**/** rĕst**/**] **50** 35

headset [hĕd**/** sĕt**/**] **83** 2

heart [härt] **5** 64

heat [hēt] **80** 27

heating pad [hē**/** tĭng păd**/**] **41** 3

hedge clippers [hĕj**/** klĭp**/** ərz] **27** 29

heel [hēl] **5** 50, **20** 5

heels [hēlz] **20** 25

height [hīt] **79** 34

helicopter [hĕl**/** ə kŏp**/** tər] **57** 2

helmet [hĕl**/** mət] **42** 12, **52** 7, **92** 14

hem [hĕm] **101** 11

hem binding [hĕm**/** bīn**/** dĭng] **101** 12

herb(s) [ürb(z)] **6** 9

(herd of) cattle [hürd**/** əv kăt**/** əl] **81** 20

high [hī] **24** 11

high blood pressure [hī**/** blŭd prĕsh**/** ər]
40 10

high chair [hī**/** chër**/**] **16** 8

high heels [hī**/** hēlz**/**] **20** 25

highway travel [hī**/** wā trăv**/** əl] **53**

hikers [hī**/** kərz] **88** 2

hiking boots [hī**/** kĭng bōōts**/**] **19** 9

hill [hĭl] **88** 4

Himalayas [hĭm**/** ə lā**/** əz] **70** 47

hind legs [hīnd**/** lĕgz**/**] **66** 3b

hip [hĭp] **4** 16

hippopotamus [hĭp**/** ə pŏt**/**ə məs]
66 14

hit [hĭt] **96** 1

hitchhiker [hĭch**/** hī**/** kər] **53** 9

hockey stick [hŏk**/** ē stĭk**/**] **92** 18

hog [hög] **66** 30

hold [hōld] **17** 12, **58** 8

hole [hōl] **94** 8

holly [hŏl**/** ē] **61** 37

holster [hōl**/** stər] **43** 8

home plate [hōm**/** plāt**/**] **93** 15

honeydew melon
[hŭn**/** ē dōō mĕl**/** ən] **9** 35

hood [hŏŏd] **51** 47

hoof [hŏŏf] **66** 35b

hoofed mammals [hŏŏft**/** măm**/** əlz] **66**

hook [hŏŏk] **32** 1, **36** 16

hook and eye [hŏŏk**/** ənd ī**/**] **101** 14

horn [hörn] **50** 12, **52** 5, **66** 16a

horse [hörs] **66** 21

horse racing [hörs**/** rā**/** sĭng] **94**

horse-drawn carriage
[hörs**/** drön kăr**/** ĭj] **54** 33

horseback rider [hörs**/** băk rī**/** dər]
87 6

horses [hörs**/** əz] **81** 23

hose [hōz] **42** 8, **50** 57

hot [hŏt] **25** 7

hot air balloon [hŏt**/** ër bə loon**/**] **57** 1

hot dog [hŏt**/** dög**/**] **18** 2

hot water faucet [hŏt**/** wŏt ər fö**/** sət]
34 17

house plants [hows**/** plănts**/**] **60** 39

household items [hows**/** hōld ī**/** təmz]
15 15

household services
[hows**/** hold sür**/** və səz] **85**

housekeeper [hows**/** kē**/** pər] **85** 8

houses [how**/** zəz] **27**

housework [hows**/** würk**/**] **38**

Huang River [hwöng**/** riv**/** ər] **71** 68

hubcap [hŭb**/** kăp**/**] **50** 36

索引

Hudson Bay [hŭd/sən bā/] **70** 18

human body [hyōō/mən bŏd/ē] **4**

hummingbird [hŭm/ĭng bürd/] **64** 2

hump [hŭmp] **67** 33a

husband [hŭz/bənd] **2** 3, **3** 12

hyacinth [hī/ə sĭnth] **60** 10

hyena [hī ē/nə] **68** 30

hypotenuse [hī pŏt/ə nōōs/] **79** 24

ice cream cone [īs/ krēm cōn/] **18** 36

ice hockey [īs/ hŏk/ē] **92**

ice pack [īs/ păk/] **41** 4

ice skates [īs/ skāts/] **19** 15

ice skating [īs/ skā/tĭng] **94**

ice tray [īs/ trā/] **30** 21

icy [ī/sē] **25** 16

Idaho [ī/də hō/] **72** 12

ignition [ĭg nĭsh/ən] **50** 14

iguana [ĭ gwŏ/nə] **65** 13

Illinois [ĭl/ə noy/] **72** 13

in [ĭn] **102** 7

in front of [ĭn frŭnt/ əv] **102** 6

in-box [ĭn/ bŏks] **83** 12

(index) finger [ĭn/ dĕks fĭng/ gər] **4** 25

Indian Ocean [ĭn/ dē ən ō/ shən/] **70** 13

Indiana [ĭn/ dē ăn/ ə] **72** 14

individual sports
 [ĭn/ də vĭj/ ōō əl spörts/] **94**

infection [ĭn fĕk/ shən] **40** 14

inflatable raft [ĭn flā/ tə bəl răft/] **59** 20

information desk
 [ĭn/ fər mā/ shən dĕsk/] **47** 22

injection [ĭn jĕk/ shən] **41** 8

injuries [ĭn/ jə rēz] **40**

insect bite [ĭn/ sĕkt bīt/] **40** 3

insects [ĭn/ sĕkts] **63**

instep [ĭn/ stĕp/] **5** 51

instruments [ĭn/ strə mənts]
 39 13, **56** 14, **98**

internal organs [ĭn tür/ nəl ör/ gənz] **5**

intersection [ĭn/ tər sĕk/ shən] **44** 11

interstate highway
 [ĭn/ tər stāt hī/ wā] **53** 1

intestines [ĭn tĕs/ tənz] **5** 67

into [ĭn/ tōō] **103** 12

Iowa [ī/ə wə] **72** 15

iris [ī/ rəs] **5** 47, **60** 11

iron (n) [ī/ ərn] **35** 12

iron (v) [ī/ ərn] **38** 11

ironing board [ī/ ər nĭng börd/] **35** 13

jack [jăk] **32** 26b, **50** 38

jacket [jăk/ ət] **19** 17, **21** 33

jackhammer [jăk/ hăm/ər] **82** 22

jail [jāl] **43** 1

janitor [jăn/ ə tər] **85** 9

jar [jär] **12** 9

jaw [jö] **4** 38

jeans [jēnz] **19** 6

jeep [jēp] **48** 9

jelly [jĕl/ ē] **18** 31

jellyfish [jĕl/ ē fĭsh/] **62** 12

jet engine [jĕt/ ĕn/ jən] **57** 11

jet fuel [jĕt/ fyōō/ əl] **80** 31

(jet) plane [jĕt/ plān/] **57** 18

jeweller [jōō/ ə lər] **84** 12

jewelry [jōō/ əl rē] **23**

jewelry box [jōō/ əl rē bŏks/] **32** 4

jigsaw [jĭg/ sö] **36** 3

jockey [jŏk/ ē] **94** 21

jogging path [jŏg/ ĭng păth/] **87** 9

judge [jŭj] **43** 10

jukebox [jōōk/ bŏks/] **16** 12

jump [jŭmp] **96** 8

jungle gym [jŭng/ əl jĭm/] **87** 17

Jupiter [jōō/ pə tər] **74** 15

jury [jōor/ ē] **43** 21

jury box [joor/ ē bŏks/] **43** 20

kangaroo [kăng/ gə rōō/] **66** 3

Kansas [kăn/ zəs] **72** 16

Kara Sea [kär/ ə sē/] **70** 31

kayak [kī/ ăk] **59** 17

Kentucky [kĕn tŭk/ ē] **72** 17

ketchup [kĕch/ əp] **16** 4

kettledrum [kĕt/ əl drŭm/] **98** 21

keyboard [kē/ börd/] **98** 1a, **100** 33

keyboard player [kē/ börd plā/ ər] **99** 22

kickstand [kĭk/ stănd/] **52** 9

kidney [kĭd/ nē] **5** 70

kidney bean(s) [kĭd/ nē bēn(z)/] **6** 13

kitchen [kĭch/ ən] **30**

kite [kīt] **91** 22

kitten [kĭt/ ən] **68** 5

knee [nē] **4** 19

knee socks [nē/ sŏks/] **22** 16

knife [nīf] **29** 15

knitting [nĭt/ ĭng] **101** 22

knitting needle [nĭt/ ĭng nē/ dəl] **101** 25

knuckle [nŭk/ əl] **4** 22

koala [kō ŏl/ ə] **66** 1

label [lā/ bəl] **46** 21

lacrosse [lə krös/] **92**

lacrosse stick [lə krös/ stĭk/] **92** 16

ladder [lăd/ ər] **42** 1, **82** 8

ladybug [lā/ dē bŭg/] **63** 14

lamb [lăm] **10** 13, **67** 24

lamp [lămp] **28** 28

lampshade [lămp/ shād/] **28** 27

landing gear [lăn/ dĭng gïr/] **57** 15

lane [lān] **94** 4

lantern [lăn/ tərn] **88** 29

lapel [lə pĕl/] **20** 1

Laptev Sea [lăp/ tĕv sē/] **70** 33

last quarter [lăst/ kwör/ tər] **74** 25

launchpad [lönch/ păd/] **75** 15

laundry [lön/ drē] **35** 28

laundry basket [lön/ drē băs/ kət] **35** 29

laundry detergent [lön/ drē də tür/ jənt]
 35 25

lawn mower [lön/ mō/ ər] **27** 12

lead guitarist [lēd/ gĭ tär/ ĭst] **99** 25

leaf [lēf] **60** 36a

leave [lēv] **77** 13

left fielder [lĕft/ fēl/ dər] **93** 1

left guard [lĕft/ gärd/] **93** 26

left lane [lĕft/ lān/] **53** 5

left tackle [lĕft/ tăk/ əl] **93** 25

leg [lĕg] **4** 17, **10** |14, **11** 20

(legal) pad [lē/ gəl păd/] **83** 26

lemon [lĕm/ ən] **8** 9

Lena River [lē/ nə rĭv/ ər] **71** 66

length [lĕngth] **79** 36

lens [lĕnz] **100** 6

leopard [lĕp/ ərd] **68** 1

letter [lĕt/ ər] **46** 7

letter carrier [lĕt/ ər kăr/ yər] **46** 3

lettuce [lĕt/ əs] **6** 6

level [lĕv/ əl] **82** 3

librarian [lī brër/ ē ən] **47** 23

library card [lī/ brër ē kärd/] **47** 3

library clerk [lī/ brër ē klürk/] **47** 1

license plate [lī/ səns plāt/] **50** 28

lid [lĭd] **30** 9

life jacket [līf/ jăk/ ət] **59** 1

life preserver [līf/ prə zür/ vər] **90** 9

lifeboat [līf/ bōt/] **58** 19, **90** 10

lifeguard [līf′ gärd′] **90** 6
lifeguard chair [līf′ gärd chër′] **90** 8
light (v) [līt] **17** 13
light (adj) [līt] **24** 9
light switch [līt′ swĭch′] **32** 25
lightbulb [līt′ bŭlb′] **35** 22
lighter [lī′ tər] **16** 30
lighthouse [līt′ hows′] **58** 14
lily [lĭl′ ē] **60** 3
lima bean(s) [lī′ mə bēn(z)′] **6** 16
lime [līm] **8** 10
line [līn] **58** 25
lines [līnz] **79**
linesman [līnz′ mən] **82** 17
lion [lī′ ən] **68** 3
lip [lĭp] **4** 43
lipstick [lĭp′ stĭk′] **23** 29
liquor (bottle) [lĭk′ ər bŏt′ əl] **16** 22
listen [lĭs′ ən] **77** 6
little finger [lĭt′ əl fĭng′ gər] **4** 28
little league baseball [lĭt′ əl lēg bās′ böl] **92**
Little Leaguer [lĭt′ əl lēg′ ər] **92** 8
little toe [lĭt′ əl tō′] **5** 55
liver [lĭv′ ər] **5** 65
livestock [līv′ stŏk′] **81** 12
living quarters [lĭv′ ĭng kwör′ tərz] **75** 11
living room [lĭv′ ĭng rōōm′] **28**
lizard [lĭz′ ərd] **65** 15
llama [lŏm′ ə] **66** 15
loaf [lōf] **12** 7
loafer [lō′ fər] **21** 42
lobby [lŏb′ ē] **44** 2
lobster [lŏb′ stər] **11** 30, **62** 13
lock [lŏk] **52** 13
locker [lŏk′ ər] **76** 6
locksmith [lŏk′ smĭth′] **85** 4
log [lög] **28** 10
long [löng] **24** 2
long johns [löng′ jönz′] **22** 7
long sleeve [löng′ slēv′] **20** 15
loose [lōōs] **24** 4
(loose-leaf) paper [lōōs′ lēf pā′ pər] **76** 13
loudspeaker [lowd′ spē′ kər] **76** 3
Louisiana [lōō ē′ zē ăn′ ə] **72** 18
lounge chair [lownj′ chër′] **27** 24

low [lō] **24** 12
lunar eclipse [lōō′ nər ĭ klĭps′] **74** 6
lunar module [lōō′ nər mŏj′ ōōl] **75** 7
lunch box [lŭnch′ bŏks′] **20** 31
lunch truck [lŭnch′ trŭk′] **49** 8
lung [lŭng] **5** 63
machine gun [mə shēn′ gŭn′] **48** 25
magazine [măg′ ə zēn′] **47** 16
magnet [măg′ nət] **78** 27
magnifying glass [măg′ nə fī ĭng glăs′] **78** 15
magnolia [măg nōl′ yə] **61** 29
mail [māl] **46** 2
mail slot [māl′ slŏt′] **46** 13
mail truck [māl′ trŭk′] **46** 5
mailbag [māl′ băg′] **46** 4
mailbox [māl′ bŏks′] **46** 1
Maine [mān] **72** 19
maintenance [mān′ tə nəns] **85**
make (the bed) [māk′ dhə bĕd′] **38** 8
makeup [māk′ ŭp′] **23**
mallet [măl′ ĭt] **36** 11
mammals [măm′ əlz] **66-69**
man [măn] **2** 2
manager [măn′ ĭ jər] **83** 18
mandolin [măn′ də lĭn′] **98** 4
mane [mān] **66** 21a
mango [măng′ gō] **8** 5
manhole [măn′ hōl′] **45** 32
mantel [măn′ təl] **28** 7
mantis [măn′ tĭs] **63** 7
manual transmission
    [măn′ yōō əl trănz mĭsh′ ən] **50**
map [măp] **70**
maple [mā′ pəl] **61** 38
marigold [măr′ ə gōld′] **60** 6
marine [mə rēn′] **48** 18
Marines [mə rēnz′] **48** 17
Mars [märz] **74** 14
Maryland [mër′ ə lənd] **72** 20
mascara [mă skăr′ ə] **23** 28
mashed potatoes [măsht′ pə tā tōz′] **18** 17
mask [măsk] **91** 35
Massachusetts [măs′ ə chōō′ sĭts] **72** 21
mast [măst] **59** 8
mat [măt] **50** 22

matches [măch′ əz] **16** 28
material [mə tir′ ē əl] **101** 4
math [măth] **79**
mattress [mă′ trəs] **32** 17
measurement [mĕzh′ ər mənt] **79**
meat [mēt] **10**
meatballs [mēt′ bölz′] **18** 11
mechanic [mə kăn′ ĭk] **84** 2
media [mē′ dē ə] **86**
medical care [mĕd′ ə kəl kër′] **39**
medicine [mĕd′ ə sən] **41**
medicine chest [mĕd′ ə sən chĕst′] **34** 14
medicine dropper [mĕd′ ə sən drŏp′ ər] **78** 26
Mediterranean Sea
    [mĕd′ ĭ tə rā′ nē ən sē′] **70** 24
melon [mĕl′ ən] **9** 35
menu [mĕn′ yōō] **16** 7
Mercury [mür′ kyə rē] **74** 11
merry-go-round [mër′ ē gō rownd′] **87** 5
message pad [mĕs′ ĭj păd′] **83** 25
messenger [mĕs′ ən jər] **86** 19
metal detector [mĕt′ əl də tĕk′ tər] **56** 10
meteor [mē′ tē ər] **74** 5
meter [mē′ tər] **55** 23
mezzanine [mĕz′ ə nēn′] **99** 13
Michigan [mĭsh′ ə gən] **72** 22
microfilm [mī′ krə fĭlm′] **47** 13
microfilm reader [mī′ krə fĭlm rē′ dər] **47** 14
microscope [mī′ krə skōp′] **78** 30
microwave oven [mī′ krə wāv ŭv′ ən] **30** 23
middle finger [mĭd′ əl fĭng′ gər] **4** 26
milk [mĭlk] **14** 5
Minicam™ [mĭn′ ē kăm′] **100** 2
Minnesota [mĭn′ ə sō′ tə] **72** 23
mirror [mir′ ər] **32** 5
Mississippi [mĭs′ ə sĭp′ ē] **72** 24
Mississippi River [mĭs′ ə sĭp′ ē rĭv′ ər] **71** 58
Missouri [mĭ zōōr′ ē] **73** 25
mitt [mĭt] **27** 20
mittens [mĭt′ ənz] **19** 11

mixed vegetables [mĭkst′ vĕj′ tə bəlz] **18** 16

mixing bowl [mĭk′ sĭng bōl′] **30** 24

mobile [mō′ bēl] **33** 2

model [mŏd′ əl] **86** 5

Mojave Desert [mō hŏv′ ē dĕz′ ərt] **71** 48

money [mŭn′ ē] **12**

money order [mŭn′ ē ör′ dər] **46** 18

monitor [mŏn′ ə tər] **100** 32

monkey [mŭng′ ke] **69** 14

monkey wrench [mŭng′ kē rĕnch′] **36** 12

monorail [mŏn′ ə rāl′] **55** 29

Montana [mŏn tăn′ ə] **73** 26

Moon [mo͞on] **74** 9

mooring [mo͝or′ ĭng] **59** 19

moose [mo͞os] **67** 35

mop [mŏp] **35** 6

(mop) refill [mŏp′ rē′ fĭl] **35** 11

mortar [mör′ tər] **48** 28

mosquito [mə skē′ tō] **63** 13

motel [mō tĕl′] **90** 3

moth [mŏth] **63** 21

mother [mŭdh′ ər] **3** 4

motor oil [mōt′ ər oyl′] **80** 33

motor scooter [mōt′ ər sko͞o′ tər] **52** 29

motorboat [mōt′ ər bōt′] **59** 13

motorcycle [mōt′ ər sī′ kəl] **52** 30, **53** 19

mountain [mown′ tən] **89** 19

mountain climbing [mown′ tən klīm′ ĭng] **89**

mountain ranges [mown′ tən rān′ jəz] **71**

mouse [mows] **66** 9

mousetrap [mows′ trăp′] **35** 32

mouth [mowth] **4** 2

mover [mo͞o′ vər] **49** 12

movie camera [mo͞o′ vē kăm′ ə rə] **100** 15

moving van [mo͞o′ vĭng văn′] **49** 11

mow [mō] **26** 6

mum [mŭm] **60** 4

muscle [mŭs′ əl] **5** 62

mushroom(s) [mŭsh′ ro͞om(z)] **7** 30

music [myo͞o′ zĭk] **99**

musical comedy [myo͞o′ zə kəl kŏm′ ə dē] **99**

musical instruments [myo͞o′ zə kəl ĭn′ strə mənts] **98**

musician [myo͞o zĭsh′ ən] **99** 10

mussel(s) [mŭs′ əl(z)] **11** 34, **62** 3

mustache [mŭs′ tăsh] **4** 40

mustard [mŭs′ tərd] **18** 1

nail [nāl] **37** 41

nail clippers [nāl′ klĭp′ ərz] **23** 31

nail polish [nāl′ pŏl′ ĭsh] **23** 25

nailbrush [nāl′ brŭsh′] **34** 20

napkin [năp′ kĭn] **29** 14

natural gas [năch′ ər əl găs′] **80** 29

Navy [nā′ vē] **48** 13

Nebraska [nə brăs′ kə] **73** 27

neck [nĕk] **4** 4

necklace [nĕk′ lĭs] **23** 6

nectarine [nĕk′ tə rēn′] **8** 17

needle [nē′ dəl] **39** 26, **60** 34a, **101** 18

needlecrafts [nē′ dəl krăfts′] **101**

needlepoint [nē′ dəl poynt′] **101** 26

neighborhood parks [nā′ bər ho͝od pärks′] **87**

nephew [nĕf′ yo͞o] **3** 13

Neptune [nĕp′ to͞on] **74** 18

nest [nĕst] **64** 31

net [nĕt] **92** 23

Nevada [nə văd′ ə] **73** 28

new [no͞o] **24** 13

New Hampshire [no͞o′ hămp′ shər] **72** 29

New Jersey [no͞o′ jür′ ze] **73** 30

New Mexico [no͞o′ mĕk′ sə kō] **73** 31

new moon [no͞o′ mo͞on′] **74** 26

New York [no͞o′ yörk′] **73** 32

newscaster [no͞oz′ kăs′ tər] **86** 2

newspaper [no͞oz′ pā′ pər] **21** 48

newsstand [no͞oz′ stănd′] **45** 30

next to [nĕkst′ to͞o] **102** 11

nickel [nĭk′ əl] **13** 28

niece [nēs] **3** 14

Niger River [nī′ jər rĭv′ ər] **71** 61

night table [nīt′ tā′ bəl] **32** 27

nightgown [nīt′ gown′] **22** 21

nightstick [nīt′ stĭk′] **43** 9

Nile River [nīl′ rĭv′ ər] **71** 63

nipple [nĭp′ əl] **33** 18

north [nörth] **71** 71

North America [nörth′ ə mĕr′ ə kə] **70** 1

North Atlantic [nörth′ ăt lăn′ tĭk] **70** 11

North Carolina [nörth′ kăr ə lī′ nə] **73** 33

North Dakota [nörth′ də kō′ tə] **73** 34

North Pacific [nörth′ pə sĭf′ ĭk] **70** 9

North Sea [nörth′ sē′] **70** 21

nose [nōz] **4** 36, **57** 8

nostril [nŏs′ trĭl] **4** 37

nozzle [nŏz′ əl] **42** 17

nuclear reactor [no͞o′ klē ər rē ăk′ tər] **80** 13

nurse [nürs] **39** 19

nut [nŭt] **37** 39

nuts [nŭts] **9**

oak [ōk] **61** 33

oar [ör] **59** 22

oarlock [ör′ lŏk′] **59** 21

oats [ōts] **60** 23

Ob River [ŏb′ rĭv′ ər] **71** 64

oboe [ō ′bō] **98** 15

obtuse angle [ŏb to͞os′ ăng′ gəl] **79** 5

occupations [ŏk′ yə pā′ shənz] **84-86**

ocean liner [ō′ shən lī′ nər] **58** 27

oceans [ō′ shənz] **70**

octopus [ŏk′ tə pəs] **62** 6

office [ö′ fĭs] **83**

office building [ö′ fĭs bĭl′ dĭng] **44** 1

officer [ö′ fĭ sər] **86** 13

Ohio [ō hī′ ō] **73** 35

oil [oyl] **38** 12

oil well [oyl′ wĕl′] **80** 1

ointment [oynt′ mənt] **41** 9

Oklahoma [ō′ klə hō′ mə] **73** 36

old [ōld] **24** 14

on [ŏn] **102** 5

on top of [ŏn tŏp′ əv] **102** 10

onion(s) [ŭn′ yən(z)] **7** 31

open [ō′ pən] **24** 15, **31** 3

optician [ŏp tĭsh′ ən] **84** 9

oral hygienist [ör′ əl hī jē′ nĭst] **39** 14

orange [ör′ ĭnj] **8** 8

orangutan [ə răng′ ə tăn′] **69** 18

orbit [ör′ bĭt] **74** 21

orchard [ör′ chərd] **81** 1

orchestra [ör′ kə strə] **99** 6

orchestra seating [ör′ kə strə sēt′ ĭng] **99** 12

orchid [ör′ kĭd] **60** 12

order [ör′ dər] **17** 5

Oregon [ör′ ə gən] **73** 37

organ [ör′ gən] **98** 29

ostrich [ŏs′ trĭch] **64** 12

otter [ŏt′ ər] **68** 10

out of [owt′ əv] **103** 7

outboard motor [owt′ börd mō′ tər] **59** 12

outer space [owt′ər spās′] **74**

outlet [owt′ lət] **36** 6

oval [ō′ vəl] **79** 18

oven [ŭv′ ən] **30** 32

over [ō′ vər] **103** 8

overalls [ō′ vər ölz′] **21** 30

overcoat [ō′ vər kōt′] **19** 20

overhead projector
[ō′ vər hĕd prə jĕk′ tər] **76** 27

overpass [ō′ vər păs′] **53** 3

owl [owl] **64** 6

oyster(s) [oy′ stər(z)] **11** 33, **62** 2

pacifier [păs′ ə fī′ ər] **33** 22

pack [păk] **13** 16

package [păk′ ĭj] **12** 4, **46** 19

pad [păd] **83** 26

paddle [păd′ əl] **59** 3, **94** 18

pail [pāl] **90** 16

paint (v) [pānt] **26** 1

paint (n) [pānt] **37** 31

paintbrush [pānt′ brŭsh′] **37** 30

Painted Desert [pān′ təd dez′ ərt] **71** 49

painter [pān′ tər] **85** 7

painting [pān′ tĭng] **28** 5

(pair of) scissors [pĕr′ əv sĭz′ ərz]
101 17

pajamas [pə jŏm′ əz] **22** 19

palm [pŏm] **4** 29, **61** 26

pan [păn] **37** 28

pancakes [păn′ kāks′] **18** 5

pancreas [pang′ krē əs] **5** 71

panda [păn də] **69** 20

panel truck [păn′ əl trŭk′] **49** 9

pansy [păn′ zē] **60** 2

panties [păn′ tēz] **22** 11

pants [pănts] **21** 27

pantyhose [păn′ tē hōz′] **22** 5

papaya [pə pī′ yə] **8** 6

paper [pā′ pər] **76** 13

paper clips [pā′ pər klĭps′] **83** 28

paper towels [pā′ pər tow′əlz] **35** 23

parachute [păr′ ə shoot′] **48** 6

parakeet [păr′ ə kēt] **64** 15

parallel lines [păr′ ə lĕl līnz′] **79** 4

paramedic [păr′ ə mĕd′ ĭk] **42** 7

Parana River [păr′ ə nŏ′ rĭv′ ər] **71** 60

parents [păr′ ənts] **2** 6

park [pärk] **87**

park ranger [pärk′ rān′ jər] **88** 5

parka [pär′ kə] **19** 8

parking lights [pär′ kĭng līts′] **51** 49

parking garage [pär′ kĭng gə rŏj′]
45 19

parking meter [pär′ kĭng mē′ tər]
45 20

parrot [păr′ ət] **64** 16

part [pärt] **4** 31

pass [păs] **96** 5

passenger [păs′ ĭn jər] **55** 25

passenger car [păs′ ĭn jər kär′] **53** 15

pasture [păs′ chər] **81** 6

patient [pā′shənt] **39** 20

patio [păt′ ē ō′] **27** 17

pattern [păt′ ərn] **101** 7

pattern piece [păt′ ərn pēs′] **101** 6

paw [pö] **69** 29a

pay [pā] **17** 7

pea(s) [pē(z)] **6** 17

peach [pēch] **9** 37

peacock [pē′ kŏk′] **64** 18

peak [pēk] **89** 20

peanut(s) [pē′ nŭt(s)′] **9** 28

pear [pĕr] **8** 18

pedal [pĕd′ əl] **39** 18, **52** 19

pedestrian [pə dĕs′ trē ən] **44** 12

peel (n) [pēl] **9** 20a

peel (v) [pēl] **31** 5

pegboard [pĕg′ börd′] **36** 15

pelican [pĕl′ ə kən] **64** 24

pencil [pĕn′ səl] **76** 24

pencil eraser [pĕn′ səl ə rā′ sər] **76** 21

pencil sharpener
[pĕn′ səl shär′ pə nər] **76** 20, **83** 30

Pennsylvania [pĕn səl vān′ yə] **73** 38

penny [pĕn′ ē] **13** 27

penguin [pĕn′ gwĭn] **64** 27

people [pē′ pəl] **2**

pepper shaker [pĕp′ ər shā′ kər] **29** 9

pepper(s) [pĕp′ ər(z)] **7** 22

percussion [pər kŭsh′ ən] **98**

perfume [pür′ fyoom] **23** 27

periodicals section
[pïr′ ē ŏd′ ə kəlz sĕk′ shən] **47** 15

periscope [pĕr′ ə skōp′] **48** 8

perpendicular lines
[pür′ pən dĭk′ yə lər līnz′] **79** 2

Persian Gulf [pür′ zhən gŭlf′] **70** 28

personal computer (PC)
[pür′ sə nəl kŭm pyoo′ tər]/
[pē′ sē′] **100** 31

personnel [pür′ sə nĕl′] **48**

petal [pĕt′ əl] **60** 18b

petri dish [pēt′ rē dĭsh′] **78** 3

petunia [pə toon′ yə] **60** 7

pharmacist [fär′ mə sĭst] **84** 1

phases of the moon
[fā′ zəz əv dhə moon′] **74**

pheasant [fĕz′ ənt] **64** 19

Phillips screwdriver
[fĭl′ ĭps skroo′ drī vər] **37** 25

phone [fōn] **32** 26

photocopier [fō′ tə kŏp′ ē ər] **83** 24

photocopy machine
[fō tə kŏp ē mə shēn′] **47** 18

photographer [fə tŏg′ rə fər] **86** 4

photography [fə tŏg′ rə fē] **100**

piano [pē ăn′ ō] **98** 1

piccolo [pĭk′ ə lō′] **98** 12

pick (v) [pĭk] **26** 7

pick (n) [pĭk] **98** 11a

pickup truck [pĭk′ ŭp trŭk′] **49** 4

pickax [pĭk′ ăks′] **82** 13

pickle [pĭk′ əl] **18** 8

picnic area [pĭk′ nĭk ër′ ē ə] **88**

picnic basket [pĭk′ nĭk băs′ kət] **88** 13

picnic table [pĭk′ nĭk tā′ bəl] **88** 15

piece [pēs] **12** 22

pier [pïr] **58** 3

pierced earring [pïrst′ ïr′ ĭng] **23** 16

pigeon [pĭj′ ən] **64** 1

pill [pĭl] **41** 7

pillow [pĭl′ ō] **32** 16

pillowcase [pĭl′ ō kās′] **32** 15

索引

pilot [pī/ lət] **56** 15

pin [pĭn] **23** 8, **94** 5, **101** 20

pincushion [pĭn/ kŏŏsh/ ən] **101** 3

pine [pīn] **60** 34

pineapple [pīn/ ăp/ əl] **8** 4

ping-pong [pĭng/ pŏng/] **94**

ping-pong ball [pĭng/ pŏng böl/] **94** 19

pinking shears [pĭng/ kĭng shïrz/]
    101 5

pipe [pīp] **16** 26, **35** 18

pipette [pī pĕt/] **78** 14

pit [pĭt] **8** 37a

pitcher [pĭch/ ər] **29** 4, **93** 12

pitcher's mound [pĭch/ ərz mownd/]
    93 11

pitchfork [pĭch/ förk/] **81** 14

pizza [pēt/ sə] **18** 30

plaid [plăd] **24** 22

plane [plān] **57** 18

planets [plăn/ əts] **74**

plant (v) [plănt] **26** 4

plants (n) [plănts] **60**

plate [plāt] **29** 13

plateau [plă tō/] **88** 1

platform [plăt/ förm/] **54** 11

playground [plā/ grownd/] **87** 15

playpen [plā/ pĕn/] **33** 30

pleasure boating [plĕzh/ ər bō/ tĭng] **59**

pliers [plī/ ərz] **36** 19

plug [plŭg] **37** 43d

plum [plŭm] **9** 34

plumber [plŭm/ ər] **85** 1

plunger [plŭn/ jər] **35** 14

Pluto [ploo/ tō] **74** 19

pocket [pŏk/ ət] **21** 41

pod [pŏd] **6** 17a

podium [pō/ dē əm] **99** 7

poinsettia [poyn sĕt/ē ə] **60** 15

poison ivy [poy/ zən ī/ vē] **61** 45

poison oak [poy/ zən ōk/] **61** 43

poison sumac [poy/ zən soo/ măk]
    61 44

poisonous plants [poy/ zə nəs plănts/]
    61

polar bear [pōl/ ər bër/] **69** 22

pole [pōl] **94** 34, **95** 14

police officer [pə lēs/ öf/ ə sər] **43** 6

police station [pə lēs/ stā/ shən] **43**

polish [pŏl/ ĭsh] **38** 3

polka dot [pō/ kə dŏt/] **24** 19

pond [pŏnd] **87** 8

pony [pō/ nē] **67** 20

poplar [pŏp/ lər] **61** 30

porch [pörch] **27** 6

porcupine [pör/ kyə pīn/] **66** 11

pork [pörk] **10** 6

pork chops [pörk/ chŏps/] **18** 15

port [pört] **58**

porter [pör/ tər] **56** 5

porthole [pört/ hōl/] **58** 21

post [pōst] **23** 18

post office [pōst/ öf/ ĭs] **44** 9, **46**

postal worker [pōs/ təl wür/ kər] **46** 14

postcard [pōst/ kärd] **46** 17

postmark [pōst/ märk/] **46** 9

pot [pŏt] **30** 13

pot holder [pŏt/ hōl/ dər] **30** 34

potato chips [pə tā/ tō chĭps/] **18** 4

potato(es) [pə tā/ tō(z)] **7** 23

potty [pŏt/ ē] **33** 33

pouch [powch] **66** 3c

pouched mammals [powcht/ măm/ əlz]
    66

poultry [pōl/ trē] **10**

pour [pör] **31** 4

power lines [pow/ ər līnz/] **80** 24

power sander [pow/ ər săn/ dər] **37** 26

power saw [pow/ ər sö/] **27** 25

power station [pow/ ər stā/ shən] **80** 20

prepositions [prep/ ə zĭ/ shənz]
    102, 103

primates [prī/ māts] **69**

print [prĭnt] **24** 21

printer [prĭn/ tər] **83** 4

printout [prĭnt/ owt/] **83** 8

prints [prĭnts] **100** 11

prism [prĭz/ əm] **78** 1

private jet [prī/ vət jĕt/] **57** 3

produce [prŏd/ oos] **14** 9

programs [prō/ grămz] **99** 17

projector [prə jĕk/ tər] **100** 16

propane gas [prō/ pān găs/] **80** 30

propeller plane [prə pĕl/ ər plān/] **57** 7

prosecuting attorney
    [prŏ/ sə kyoo tĭng ə tür/ nē] **43** 17

prune [proon] **9** 22

public library [pŭb/ lĭk lī/ brër ē] **47**

public transportation
    [pŭb/ lĭk trăns pər tā/ shən] **54**

public telephone [pŭb/ lĭk tĕl/ ə fōn]
    44 7

puck [pŭk] **92** 17

pump [pŭmp] **13** 14, **52** 21

pumpkin [pŭmp/ kĭn] **7** 26

punishment [pŭn/ ĭsh mənt] **43**

pupil [pyoo/ pəl] **5** 48

puppy [pŭp/ ē] **69** 27

purse [pürs] **20** 23

push [pŏŏsh] **26** 12

putter [pŭt/ ər] **94** 9

puzzle [pŭz/ əl] **33** 31

pyramid [pïr/ ə mĭd/] **79** 25

quantities [kwŏn/ tə tēz] **12**

quarter [kwör/ tər] **11** 18, **13** 30,
    79 31

quarterback [kwör/ tər băk/] **93** 32

quill [kwĭl] **66** 11a

quilting [kwĭl/ tĭng] **101** 32

rabbit [răb/ ĭt] **66** 13

raccoon [ră koon/] **68** 7

race track [rās/ trăk/] **95**

(racing) handlebars
    [rā/ sĭng hăn/ dəl bärz] **52** 2

rack [răk] **47** 17, **78** 8

racket [răk/ ĭt] **94** 2

racquet [răk/ ĭt] **94** 29

racquetball [răk/ ĭt böl/] **94** 30

radiator [rā/ dē āt/ ər] **51** 56

radio [rā/ dē ō/] **50** 18

radish(es) [răd/ ĭsh (əz)] **7** 29

radius [rā/ dē əs] **79** 14

raft [răft] **89** 16

rafters [răf/ tərz] **82** 1

rafting [răf/ tĭng] **89**

rags [răgz] **35** 4

rain boots [rān/ boots/] **19** 25

raincoat [rān/ kōt/] **21** 38

rainy [rān/ ē] **25** 1

raise (one's hand) [rāz/ wŭnz hănd/]
    77 1

raisin(s) [rā/ zən(z)] **9** 24

rake (v) [rāk] **26** 10

rake (n) [rāk] **27** 30

ranch [rănch] **81**

ranch house [rănch′ hows′] **27**

ranching [rănch′ ĭng] **81**

rapids [răp′ ĭdz] **89** 17

rash [răsh] **40** 1

raspberries [răz′ bër′ ēz] **8** 16

rat [răt] **66** 7

rattle [răt′ əl] **33** 21

rattlesnake [răt′ əl snāk′] **65** 10

razor [rā′ zər] **23** 20

razor blades [rā′ zər blādz′] **23** 23

read [rēd] **77** 4

real estate agent [rēl′ ə stāt ā′ jənt]
    85 5

rear bumper [rïr′ bŭm′ pər] **50** 42

rearview mirror [rïr′ vyōō mïr′ ər]
    50 7

receipt [rə sēt′] **15** 20, **55** 24

receiver [rə sē′ vər] **100** 21

receptionist [rə sĕp′ shə nəst] **86** 17

recliner [rə klī′ nər] **28** 16

records [rĕk′ ərdz] **100** 23

rectangle [rĕk′ tăng′ gəl] **79** 19

Red Sea [rĕd′ sē′] **70** 29

redwood [rĕd′ wŏŏd′] **61** 25

(reel of) film [rēl′ əv fĭlm′] **100** 17

referee [rĕf′ ə rē′] **93** 22, **94** 16

reference section
    [rĕf′ ə rəns sĕk′ shən] **47** 21

(reference) librarian
    [rĕf′ ə rəns lī brër′ e ən] **47** 23

refill [rē′ fĭl′] **35** 11

refinery [rə fī′ nə rē] **80** 12

reflector [rə flĕk′ tər] **52** 25

refreshment stand
    [rə frĕsh′ mənt stănd′] **90** 2

refrigerator [rə frĭj′ ə rā′ tər] **30** 19

reins [rānz] **94** 22

relationships [rə lā′ shən ships′] **2**

remedies [rĕm′ ə dēz] **41**

remote control [rə mōt′ kən trōl′]
    28 17

repair [rə për′] **38** 10

repairperson [rə për′ pür′ sən] **84** 5

reporter [rə pör′ tər] **86** 11

reptiles [rĕp′ tīlz] **65**

rescue [rĕs′ kyōō] **42**

restaurant [rĕs′ tə rənt] **16**

retriever [rə trē′ vər] **69** 26

return address [rə türn′ ă drĕs′] **46** 8

rhinoceros [rī nŏs′ ə rəs] **66** 16

Rhode Island [rōd′ ī′ lənd] **73** 39

rice [rīs] **60** 21

ride [rīd] **97** 13

rider [rī′ dər] **54** 6

rifle [rī′ fəl] **48** 21

right angle [rīt′ ăng′ gəl] **79** 23

right fielder [rīt′ fēl′ dər] **93** 3

right guard [rīt′ gärd′] **93** 28

right lane [rīt′ lān′] **53** 7

right tackle [rīt′ tăk′ əl] **93** 29

right triangle [rīt′ trī′ ăng gəl] **79** 22

rind [rīnd] **8** 8b

ring(s) [rĭng(z)] **23** 2, **74** 16a, **94** 17

ring binder [rĭng′ bīn′ dər] **76** 14

ring finger [rĭng′ fĭng′ gər] **4** 27

ring stand [rĭng′ stănd′] **78** 19

rink [rĭngk] **94** 25

Rio Grande River [rē′ ō grănd′ rĭv′ ər]
    71 57

rivers [riv′ ərz] **71**

road sign [rōd′ sīn′] **53** 23

road work [rōd′ würk′] **82**

roadrunner [rōd′ rŭn′ ər] **64** 32

roast [rōst] **10** 3, **10** 8

roasting pan [rōs′ tĭng păn′] **30** 17

robes [rōbz] **43** 11

robin [rŏb′ in] **64** 9

rock group [rŏk′ grōōp′] **99**

rocket [rŏk′ ət] **75** 13

rocking chair [rŏk′ ĭng chër′] **33** 16

rocks [rŏks] **88** 11

Rocky Mountains [rŏk′ ē mown′ tənz]
    71 40

rodents [rō′ dənts] **66**

roll [rōl] **12** 11, **18** 19

(roll of) film [rōl′ əv fĭlm′] **100** 10

roller [rōl′ ər] **37** 29

rolling pin [rōl′ ĭng pĭn′] **30** 25

rolodex [rōl′ ə dĕks′] **83** 14

roof [rōōf] **27** 4

rooster [rōō′ stər] **64** 21

root [rōōt] **60** 35d

rope [rōp] **89** 23

rose [rōz] **60** 18

rotor [rō′ tər] **57** 2a

rough [rŭf] **95** 6

router [row′ tər] **37** 37

row [rō] **47** 11, **81** 18

rowboat [rō′ bōt′] **59** 23

Rub′ al Khali Desert
    [rōōb′ ăl kŏl′ ē dĕz′ ərt] **71** 52

rubber tubing [rŭb′ ər tōōb′ ĭng] **78** 18

rudder [rŭd′ ər] **59** 5

rug [rŭg] **32** 28

ruler [rōō′ lər] **76** 23

run [rŭn] **96** 6

rung [rŭng] **82** 9

runner [rŭn′ ər] **91** 23, **94** 31

runway [rŭn′ wā′] **57** 19

saddle [săd′ əl] **94** 20

safety glasses [săf′ tē glăs′ əz] **78** 12

safety goggles [săf′ tē gŏg′ əlz] **94** 28

safety pin [săf′ tē pĭn′] **33** 11

Sahara Desert [sə hër′ ə dĕz′ ərt]
    71 51

sail [sāl] **59** 9

sailboard [sāl′ börd′] **59** 15

sailboat [sāl′ bōt′] **59** 4

sailor [sāl′ ər] **48** 14

salad bowl [săl′ əd bōl′] **29** 25

salad dressing [săl′ əd drĕs′ ĭng] **18** 12

salamander [săl′ ə măn′ dər] **65** 14

salesperson [sālz′ pür′ sən] **86** 12

salt shaker [sölt′ shā′ kər] **29** 10

sand (v) [sănd] **26** 14

sand (n) [sănd] **90** 31

sand dunes [sănd′ dōōnz′] **90** 12

sand trap [sănd′ trăp′] **95** 11

sandal [săn′ dəl] **20** 19

sandbox [sănd′ bŏks′] **87** 13

sandcastle [sănd′ kăs′ əl] **91** 32

sandpaper [sănd′ pā′ pər] **37** 27

sandwich [sănd′ wĭch] **16** 16

sanitation worker
    [săn ə tā′ shən wür′ kər] **49** 7

Saturn [săt′ ərn] **74** 16

saucepan [sös′ păn′] **30** 8

saucer [sö′ sər] **29** 21

sausage [sö′ sĭj] **10** 7

saw [sö] **36** 8

saxophone [săk′ sə fōn′] **98** 24

scaffolding [skăf′ əl dĭng] **82** 7

scale [skāl] **14** 7, **34** 32, **78** 4

scallop(s) [skăl′ əp(s)] **11** 35, **62** 10

scarecrow [skër'krō'] **81** 19

scarf [skärf] **19** 19

scenery [sē'nə rē] **99** 2

school [skool] **76, 77**

science lab [sī'əns lăb'] **78**

scissors [sĭz'ərz] **101** 17

scoreboard [skör'börd'] **93** 19

scorpion [skör'pē ən] **63** 8

scouring pad [skowr'ĭng păd'] **30** 11

scrape [skrāp] **26** 15

scraper [skrāp'ər] **36** 14

screen [skrēn] **27** 19, **100** 14

screw [skroo] **37** 42

screwdriver [skroo'drī'vər] **37** 24

scrub [skrŭb] **38** 2

scuba tank [skoo'bə tăngk'] **91** 37

sea gull [sē'gŭl'] **64** 4

sea horse [sē'hörs'] **65** 1

Sea of Japan [sē'əv jə păn'] **70** 36

Sea of Okhotsk [sē'əv ō kŏtsk']
70 35

seafood [sē'food'] **10**

seal [sēl] **68** 12

seam [sēm] **101** 10

seas [sēz] **70**

seat [sēt] **52** 16, **54** 2

seat belt [sēt'bĕlt'] **50** 23

second baseman [sĕk'ənd bās'mən]
93 7

secretary [sĕk'rə tër'ē] **83** 11

section [sĕk'shən] **8** 8a, **79** 15

security [sə kyoor'ə tē] **56**

security guard [sə kyoor'ə tē gärd']
56 9, **86** 14

sedan [sə dăn'] **51**

seed [sēd] **8** 8c

seesaw [sē'sö'] **87** 18

serve [sürv] **17** 3, **96** 2

service area [sür'vəs ër'ē ə] **53** 11

sevice court [sür'vəs kört'] **95** 1

service line [sür'vəs līn'] **95** 3

set (the table) [sĕt'dhə tā'bəl] **17** 8

sewing [sō'ĭng] **101**

sewing machine [sō'ĭng mə shēn']
101 1

shade [shād] **33** 1

shaft [shăft] **80** 10

shampoo [shăm poo'] **34** 8

shank [shănk] **37** 43b

shark [shärk] **65** 5

shaving cream [shā'vĭng krēm'] **23** 22

sheep [shēp] **67** 25, **81** 10

sheet [shēt] **32** 19

sheet music [shēt'myoo'zĭk] **98** 2

shelf [shĕlf] **14** 6, **47** 26

shell [shĕl] **48** 27, **62** 1a, **65** 18a,
90 40

shellfish [shĕl'fĭsh'] **11**

shepherd [shĕp'ərd] **69** 28

shingle [shĭng'gəl] **82** 2

ship [shĭp] **58** 9

shirt [shürt] **21** 46

shock absorbers [shŏk'əb zör'bərz]
52 31

shoe [shoo] **21** 49

shoelace [shoo'lās'] **20** 7

shoot [shoot] **97** 16

shop worker [shŏp'wür'kər] **85** 12

shopping bag [shŏp'ĭng băg'] **20** 18

shopping basket [shŏp'ĭng băs'kət]
14 8

shopping cart [shŏp'ĭng kärt'] **15** 19

short [shört] **24** 1

short sleeve [shört'slēv'] **20** 21

shorts [shörts] **20** 14

shortstop [shört'stŏp'] **93** 5

shoulder [shōl'dər] **4** 5, **53** 22

(shoulder) bag [shōl'dər băg'] **21** 35

shovel (n) [shŭv'əl] **27** 31, **82** 15,
90 17

shovel (v) [shŭv'əl] **26** 13

shower cap [show'ər kăp'] **34** 3

shower curtain [show'ər kür'tən] **34** 5

shower head [show'ər hĕd'] **34** 4

shrimp [shrĭmp] **11** 31, **62** 8

shutter [shŭt'ər] **27** 8

shuttle car [shŭt'əl kär'] **80** 8

side [sīd] **79** 10

side mirror [sīd'mĭr'ər] **50** 2

sideburn [sīd'bürn'] **4** 33

sidewalk [sīd'wök'] **45** 25

Sierra Madre [sē ër'ə mö'drē] **71** 42

silo [sī'lō] **81** 4

silverware [sĭl'vər wër'] **29** 22

simple animals [sĭm'pəl ăn'ə məlz] **62**

singer [sĭng'ər] **99** 24

sink [sĭngk] **34** 19

sister [sĭs'tər] **3** 10

sister-in-law [sĭs'tər ən lö'] **3** 8

six-pack [sĭks'păk'] **13** 13

skate (n) [skāt] **94** 26

skate (v) [skāt] **97** 9

skein [skān] **101** 24

ski [skē] **95** 17

ski boot [skē'boot'] **95** 15

ski cap [skē'kăp'] **19** 16

ski lift [skē'lĭft'] **95** 18

ski slope [skē'slōp'] **95**

skier [skē'ər] **94** 35

skin [skĭn] **9** 37b

skirt [skürt] **21** 36

skis [skēz] **94** 33

skunk [skŭngk] **68** 8

slacks [slăks] **20** 4

sleeping bag [slē'pĭng băg'] **89** 26

sleepwear [slēp'wër'] **22**

slice (n) [slīs] **13** 21

slice (v) [slīs] **31** 10

slide [slīd] **78** 31, **87** 12

slide projector [slīd'prə jĕk'tər]
100 13

slides [slīdz] **100** 12

sling [slĭng] **39** 3

slippers [slĭp'ərz] **22** 18

slug [slŭg] **62** 4

small [smöl] **24** 7

smoke [smōk] **42** 15

smoke detector [smōk'də tĕk'tər]
33 15

smokestack [smök'stăk'] **58** 18,
80 22

snacks [snăks] **14** 18

snail [snāl] **62** 1

snake [snāk] **65** 9

snap [snăp] **101** 13

sneakers [snē'kərz] **20** 11

snorkel [snör'kəl] **91** 34

snow plow [snō'plow'] **49** 5

snowy [snō'e] **25** 3

soap [sōp] **34** 15

soap dish [sōp'dĭsh'] **34** 6

soccer [sŏk'ər] **92**

soccer ball [sŏk'ər böl'] **92** 26

socks [sŏks] **22** 17

sofa [sōʹ fə] **28** 25

soft drink [söftʹ drĭngkʹ] **16** 11

softball [söftʹ bölʹ] **92, 92** 10

solar collector [sōʹ lər kə lĕkʹ tər]
80 17

solar eclipse [sōʹ lər ĭ klĭpsʹ] **74** 10

solar system [sōʹ lər sĭsʹ təm] **74**

soldier [sōlʹ jər] **48** 16

sole [sōl] **20** 6

solid [sŏlʹ əd] **24** 20

solid figures [sŏlʹ əd fĭgʹ yərz] **79**

son [sŭn] **3** 16

Sony Walkman [sōʹ nē wökʹ mən]
100 30

sorc throat [sörʹ thrōtʹ] **40** 12

south [sowth] **71** 72

South America [sowthʹ ə mërʹ ə kə]
70 2

South Atlantic [sowthʹ ăt lănʹ tək]
70 12

South Carolina [sowthʹ kăr ə līʹ nə]
73 40

South China Sea [sowthʹ chiʹ nə sēʹ]
70 39

South Dakota [sowthʹ də kōʹ tə] **73** 41

South Pacific [sowth pə sĭfʹ ək] **70** 10

space probe [spāsʹ prōb] **75** 4

space program [spāsʹ prōʹ grăm] **75**

space shuttle [spāsʹ shŭtʹ əl] **75** 14

space station [spāsʹ stāʹ shən] **75** 1

space suit [spāsʹ sōotʹ] **75** 6

spacecraft [spāsʹ krăftʹ] **75**

spaghetti [spə gĕtʹ ē] **18** 10

spaniel [spănʹ yəl] **69** 24

spare ribs [spërʹ rĭbzʹ] **10** 10

spare tire [spërʹ tīrʹ] **51** 39

sparrow [spărʹ ō] **64** 10

spatula [spăchʹə lə] **27** 21

speaker [spēʹ kər] **28** 21, **100** 24

speed limit sign [spēdʹ lĭm ət sīnʹ]
53 8

speedometer [spə dŏmʹ ə tər] **50** 10

spider [spīʹ dər] **63** 16

spinach [spĭnʹ əch] **6** 8

spinal cord [spīʹ nəl kördʹ] **5** 58

spiral notebook [spīʹ rəl nōtʹ bŏok]
76 15

split [splĭt] **11** 17

split end [splĭtʹ ĕndʹ] **93** 24

spoke [spōk] **52** 26

sponge [spŭnj] **34** 7

(sponge) mop [spŭnjʹ mŏpʹ] **35** 6

(spool of) thread [spōolʹ əv thrĕdʹ]
101 2

spoon [spōon] **29** 8

sports car [spörtsʹ kärʹ] **53** 17

sports [spörts] **92-97**

spotlight [spŏtʹ lītʹ] **99** 4

sprain [sprān] **40** 13

spray can [sprāʹ kănʹ] **13** 24

spray starch [sprāʹ stärchʹ] **35** 21

spread [sprĕd] **17** 11

Spring [sprĭng] **26**

sprinkler [sprĭngʹ klər] **27** 13, **87** 14

sprocket [sprŏkʹ ət] **52** 20

square [skwër] **79** 9

squid [skwĭd] **62** 5

squirrel [skwürʹ əl] **66** 10

stage [stāj] **99** 5

staircase [stërʹ kās] **28** 12

stakc [stāk] **89** 30

stamp [stămp] **46** 10

stands [stăndz] **93** 10

staple remover [stāpʹ əl rə mooʹ vər]
83 29

stapler [stāpʹ lər] **83** 27

star [stär] **74** 4

starfish [stärʹ fĭshʹ] **62** 7

starting gate [stärʹ tĭng gātʹ] **95** 20

station [stāʹ shən] **55** 18

station wagon [stāʹ shən wăgʹ ən] **50**

steak [stāk] **10** 5, **11** 29, **18** 21

steam [stēm] **31** 12

steamer [stēmʹ ər] **30** 3

steering wheel [stürʹ ĭng wēlʹ] **50** 8

stem [stĕm] **8** 2a, **60** 1a

step [stĕp] **28** 13

stepladder [stĕpʹ lădʹ ər] **35** 1

stereo cassette player
[stĕrʹ ē ō kə sĕt plāʹ ər] **100** 25

stereo system [stĕrʹ ē ō sĭsʹ təm] **28** 20

stern [stürn] **58** 11

stethoscope [stĕthʹ ə skōpʹ] **39** 9

stewing meat [stooʹ ĭng mēt] **10** 4

stick [stĭk] **12** 5

stick shift [stĭkʹ shĭftʹ] **50** 24

sting [stĭng] **63** 8a

stingray [stĭngʹ rāʹ] **65** 6

stir [stür] **31** 1

stitch [stĭch] **101** 19

stitches [stĭchʹ əz] **39** 21

stockings [stŏkʹ ĭngz] **22** 6

stomach [stŭmʹ ək] **5** 66

stomachache [stŭmʹ ək ākʹ] **40** 7

stool [stōol] **78** 34

stopper [stŏpʹ ər] **34** 10, **78** 10

stork [störk] **64** 30

stove [stōv] **30** 30

straight line [strātʹ līnʹ] **79** 1

(strand of) beads [străndʹ əv bēdzʹ]
23 7

strap [străp] **54** 8

straw [strö] **16** 10

strawberry [ströʹ bërʹ ē] **8** 15

strawberry shortcake
[ströʹ bër ē shörtʹ kāk] **18** 26

stream [strēm] **88** 6

street [strēt] **45** 31

street cleaner [strētʹ klēʹ nər] **49** 1

street sign [strētʹ sīnʹ] **44** 8

streetcar [strētʹ kärʹ] **55** 30

streetlight [strētʹ lītʹ] **45** 29

stretch [strĕch] **95** 19

stretch bandage [strĕchʹ bănʹ dĭj]
40 13a

strctcher [strĕchʹ ər] **39** 12

stretchie [strĕchʹ ē] **33** 19

string [strĭng] **46** 20, **98** 10a

string bean(s) [strĭngʹ bēn(z)ʹ] **6** 15

strings [strĭngz] **98**

striped [strīpt] **24** 17

stroller [strōʹ lər] **33** 14

student [stōoʹ dənt] **76** 19

stuffed animal [stŭftʹ ăn ə məl] **33** 27

subject [sŭbʹ jəkt] **47** 10

submarine [sŭbʹ mə rēnʹ] **48** 7

subway [sŭbʹ wāʹ] **54**

subway station [sŭbʹ wā stāʹ shən]
44 16

sugar (packet) [shōogʹ ər păkʹ ət] **16** 13

sugar bowl [shōogʹ ər bōlʹ] **29** 23

sugarcane [shōogʹ ər kānʹ] **60** 20

suitcase [sōotʹ kāsʹ] **56** 7

Summer [sŭmʹ ər] **26**

索引

sun [sŭn] **74** 7, **80** 3

sunbather [sŭn**/** bā**/** dhər] **90** 19

sundae [sŭn**/** dē] **18** 23

sunflower [sŭn**/** flŏw**/** ər] **60** 19

sunglasses [sŭn**/** glăs**/** əz] **90** 14

sunny [sŭn**/** ē] **25** 4

(sunnyside-up) egg
   [sŭn**/** ē sīd ŭp**/** ĕg**/**] **18** 32

sunroof [sŭn**/** roof**/**] **51** 44

suntan lotion [sŭn**/** tăn lō**/** shən] **91** 39

supermarket [soo**/** pər mär**/** kət] **14**

surf [sürf] **97** 12

surfboard [sürf**/** börd**/**] **91** 25

surgery [sŭr**/** jə rē] **41** 2

suspect [sŭs**/** pĕkt] **43** 3

swan [swŏn] **64** 28

sweatband [swĕt**/** bănd**/**] **20** 12

sweater [swĕt**/** ər] **19** 7, **19** 13, **19** 23

sweatpants [swĕt**/** pănts**/**] **20** 10

sweatshirt [swĕt**/** shürt**/**] **20** 8

sweep [swēp] **38** 7

swimmer [swĭm**/** ər] **91** 28

swing [swĭng] **33** 24

swings [swĭngz] **87** 16

switch [swĭch] **37** 43c

switchboard [swĭch**/** börd**/**] **83** 3

switchboard operator
   [swĭch**/** börd ŏp**/** ə rā tər] **83** 1

swordfish [sörd**/** fĭsh**/**] **65** 3

synthesizer [sĭn**/** thə sī**/** zər] **99** 21

syringe [sə rĭnj**/**] **39** 27

syrup [sĭr**/** əp] **18** 6

T-shirt [tē**/** shürt**/**] **21** 29

table [tā**/** bəl] **29** 7

tablecloth [tā**/** bəl klŏth**/**] **29** 16

tablet [tăb**/** lət] **41** 6

taco [tŏ**/** kō] **18** 24

tadpole [tăd**/** pōl**/**] **65** 16

tail [tāl] **57** 10, **65** 3a, **66** 3a

taillight [tāl**/** līt**/**] **50** 31

tailor [tā**/** lər] **84** 6

take [tāk] **17** 10

takeoff [tāk**/** ŏf**/**] **57**

Takla Makan Desert
   [tŏk**/** lə mə kŏn**/** dĕz**/** ərt] **71** 53

tambourine [tăm**/** bə rēn**/**] **98** 17

tank [tăngk] **48** 10

tank top [tăngk**/** tŏp**/**] **20** 13

tanker [tăngk**/** ər] **58** 15

tap [tăp] **16** 20

tape [tāp] **46** 22

tape measure [tāp**/** mĕzh**/** ər] **36** 21, **101** 15

taxi [tăk**/** sē] **55**

taxi stand [tăk**/** sē stănd**/**] **55** 28

taxicab [tăk**/** sē kăb**/**] **55** 27

tea [tē] **16** 15

teacher [tē**/** chər] **76** 4

teakettle [tē**/** kĕt**/** əl] **30** 28

team sports [tēm**/** spörts**/**] **92**

teapot [tē**/** pŏt**/**] **29** 19

tear [tër] **77** 9

teddy bear [tĕd**/** ē bër**/**] **33** 3

tee [tē] **95** 13

telephone [tĕl**/** ə fōn**/**] **83** 15

telescope [tĕl**/** ə skōp**/**] **74** 22

television [tĕl**/** ə vĭzh**/** ən] **28** 18, **100** 5

teller [tĕl**/** ər] **86** 15

temperature [tĕm**/** pər ə chər] **25** 6

Tennessee [tĕn**/** ə sē**/**] **73** 42

tennis [tĕn**/** əs] **94**

tennis ball [tĕn**/** əs böl**/**] **94** 1

tennis court [tĕn**/** əs kört**/**] **95**

tent [tĕnt] **89** 24

tentacle [tĕn**/** tə kəl] **62** 12a

terminal [türm**/** ə nəl] **51** 55, **58** 29

terminal building [türm**/** ə nəl bĭl**/** dĭng] **57** 16

termite [tür**/** mīt] **63** 11

terrier [tĕr**/** ē ər] **69** 25

test tube [tĕst**/** toob**/**] **78** 9

Texas [tĕk**/** səs] **73** 43

textbook [tĕkst**/** book**/**] **76** 26

theater [thē**/** ə tər] **99**

thermometer
   [thər möm**/** ə tər] **25** 5, **78** 22

thermos [thür**/** məs] **88** 14

thigh [thī] **4** 18, **11** 19

thimble [thĭm**/** bəl] **101** 21

third (1/3) [thürd] **79** 32

third baseman [thürd**/** bās**/** mən] **93** 4

thorn [thörn] **60** 18c

thread [thrĕd] **37** 42b, **101** 2

three-piece suit [thrē**/** pēs soot] **21** 40

throat [thrōt] **5** 59

through [throo] **103** 1

throw [thrō] **97** 10

thumb [thŭm] **4** 24

thumbtack [thŭm**/** tăk**/**] **76** 25

ticket [tĭk**/** ət] **55** 16, **56** 4

ticket window [tĭk**/** ət wĭn**/** dō] **55** 19

tie (n) [tī] **21** 47

tie (v) [tī] **77** 12

tie clip [tī**/** klĭp**/**] **23** 14

tie pin [tī**/** pĭn**/**] **23** 13

tiger [tī**/** gər] **68** 2

tight [tīt] **24** 3

tighten [tī**/** tən] **38** 4

tight end [tīt**/** ĕnd**/**] **93** 30

tights [tīts] **19** 14

tile [tīl] **34** 27

timer [tī**/** mər] **78** 13

timetable [tīm**/** tā**/** bəl] **55** 20

tip [tĭp] **55** 22

tire [tīr] **50** 37, **52** 28

tissues [tĭsh**/** ooz] **32** 13

title [tī**/** təl] **47** 9

to [too] **103** 9

toast [tōst] **18** 34

toaster [tōs**/** tər] **30** 16

toe [tō] **5** 54

toenail [tō**/** nāl**/**] **5** 56

toilet [toy**/** lət] **34** 29

toilet brush [toy**/** lət brŭsh**/**] **34** 31

toilet paper [toy**/** lət pā**/** pər] **34** 30

toiletries [toy**/** lə trēz] **23**

token booth [tō**/** kən booth**/**] **54** 13

tollbooth [tōl**/** booth**/**] **53** 27

tomato(es) [tə mā**/** tō(z)] **7** 19

tongs [tŏngz] **78** 29

tongue [tŭng] **4** 41

tongue depressor [tŭng**/** də prĕs**/** ər] **40** 12a

toolbox [tool**/** bŏks**/**] **36** 23

toolshed [tool**/** shĕd**/**] **27** 28

tooth [tooth] **4** 42

toothache [tooth**/** āk**/**] **40** 9

toothbrush [tooth**/** brŭsh**/**] **34** 21

toothless mammals [tooth**/** ləs măm**/** əlz] **66**

toothpaste [tooth**/** pāst**/**] **34** 16

tortoise [tör**/** təs] **65** 18

tossed salad [töst**/** săl**/** əd] **18** 13

touch [tŭch] **77** 2

touring handlebars
[tŏŏr/ ĭng hăn/ dəl bärz] **52** 12

tow truck [tō/ trŭk] **49** 2

toward [törd] **103** 4

towel rack [tow/ əl răk/] **34** 25

towrope [tō/ rōp/] **59** 11

toy chest [toy/ chĕst/] **33** 29

track [trăk] **54** 10, **94** 32

track and field [trăk/ ənd fēld/] **94**

tractor [trăk/ tər] **81** 15

tractor trailer [trăk/ tər trā/ lər] **49** 15

traffic cop [trăf/ ək kŏp/] **44** 10

traffic light [trăf/ ək līt/] **45** 21

trailer [trā/ lər] **53** 10

train [trān] **55**

training wheels [trān/ ĭng wēlz/] **52** 1

transcript [trăn/ skrĭpt] **43** 15

transfer [trăns/ fər] **54** 4

transformer [trăns för/ mər] **80** 25

transmission towers
[trănz mĭsh/ ən tow/ ərz] **80** 23

transportation [trăns/ pər tā/ shən] **54**

transporter [trăns/ pör tər] **49** 17

trash basket [trăsh/ băs/ kət] **44** 15

trash can [trăsh/ kăn/] **87** 11

travel agent [trăv/ əl ā/ jənt] **84** 4

traveler [trăv/ ə lər] **56** 3

tray [trā] **16** 33

tray table [trā/ tā/ bəl] **56** 22

treatments [trēt/ mənts] **41**

tree [trē] **61** 35

trees [trēz] **60**

triangle [trī/ ăng/ gəl] **79** 6

tricycle [trī/ sĭ kəl] **52** 6

trigger [trĭg/ ər] **48** 22

trim [trĭm] **26** 8

tripod [trī/ pod] **100** 9

trombone [trŏm bōn/] **98** 23

trough [tröf] **81** 25

trout [trowt] **65** 2

trowel [trow/ əl] **27** 27

truck [trŭk] **49**, **53** 25

truck driver [trŭk/ drī/ vər] **49** 16

trumpet [trŭm/ pət] **98** 25

trunk [trŭngk] **51** 40, **61** 35b, **66** 17a

tub [tŭb] **12** 6

tuba [tōō/ bə] **98** 27

tube [tōōb] **13** 15, **91** 29

tugboat [tŭg/ bōt/] **58** 13

tulip [tōō/ ləp] **60** 1

turkey [tür/ kē] **10** 23, **64** 20

turnip [tür/ nəp] **7** 34

turn signal lever [türn/ sĭg nəl lĕ/ vər]
50 11

turn signal lights [türn/ sĭg nəl līts/]
51 50

turnstile [türn/ stīl/] **54** 12

turntable [türn/ tā/ bəl] **100** 18

turtle [tür/ təl] **65** 12

(turtleneck) sweater
[tür/ təl nĕk swĕ/ tər] **19** 13

tusk [tŭsk] **66** 17b

TV antenna [tē/ vē ăn tĕn/ ə] **27** 3

tweezers [twē/ zərz] **78** 32

twig [twĭg] **61** 33a

(two-door) sedan [tōō/ dör sə dăn/] **51**

type [tīp] **77** 10

typewriter [tīp/ rī/ tər] **83** 10

typing chair [tī/ pĭng chër/] **83** 17

typist [tī/ pəst] **83** 6

U.S. mailbox [yōō/ ĕs māl/ bŏks] **46** 6

U.S. Postal System
[yōō/ ĕs pōs/ təl sĭs təm] **46**

ukulele [yōō/ kə lā/ lē] **98** 3

umbrella [ŭm brĕl/ ə] **20** 24

umpire [ŭm/ pīr] **92** 1, **93** 17

uncle [ŭng/ kəl] **3** 3

under [ŭn/ dər] **102** 8

underpants [ŭn/ dər pănts/] **22** 3

undershirt [ŭn/ dər shürt/] **22** 1

underwear [ŭn/ dər wër/] **22**

uniform [yōō/ nə förm/] **21** 45, **92** 9

United States of America
[yōō nī/ təd stāts/ əv əmër/ ə kə] **72**

universe [yōō/ nə vürs/] **74**

up [ŭp] **103** 11

upper arm [ŭp/ ər ärm/] **4** 7

Urals [yōōr/ əlz] **71** 46

uranium rods [yōō rā/ nē əm rŏdz/]
80 15

Uranus [yōōr/ ə nəs] **74** 17

usher [ŭsh/ ər] **99** 16

Utah [yōō/ tö] **73** 44

utility pole [yōō tĭl/ ə tē pōl/] **80** 26

utility room [yōō tĭl/ ə tē rōōm] **35**

索引

(V-neck) sweater [vē/ nĕk swĕt/ ər]
19 23

vacuum [văk/ yōōm] **38** 14

vacuum cleaner [văk/ yōōm klē/ nər]
35 16

valve [vălv] **52** 27

van [văn] **53** 26

vase [vās] **28** 6

VCR (videocassette recorder)
[vē/ sē är/]/
[vĭd/ ē ō kə sĕt/ rə kör/ dər] **100** 4

vegetables [vĕj/ tə bəlz] **6**

vehicles and equipment
[vē/ ə kəlz ənd ə kwĭp/ mənt] **48**

vein [vān] **5** 68

vendor [vĕn/ dər] **87** 3

vent [vĕnt] **50** 21

Venus [vē/ nəs] **74** 12

verbs [vürbz] **17**, **26**, **31**, **38**, **77**, **96**

Vermont [vür mŏnt/] **73** 45

vest [vĕst] **21** 39

video [vĭd/ē ō] **100**

video camera [vĭd/ ē ō kăm/ ə rə]
100 1

videocassette (tape)
[vĭd/ ē ō kə sĕt/ tāp/] **100** 3

vine [vīn] **61** 42

viola [vē ōl/ ə] **98** 8

violet [vī/ ə lət] **60** 16

violin [vī ə lĭn/] **98** 7

Virginia [vər jĭn/ yə] **73** 46

vise [vīs] **37** 36

visor [vĭz/ ər] **50** 5

volleyball [vŏl/ ē böl/] **92**, **92** 22

waders [wā/ dərz] **88** 10

waist [wāst] **4** 13

waiter [wā tər] **16** 5

waitress [wā/ trəs] **16** 2

walk [wök] **77** 8

walker [wök/ ər] **33** 23

wall [wöl] **28** 3

wall unit [wöl/ yōō/ nət] **28** 19

wall-to-wall carpeting
[wöl/ tə wöl kär/ pə tĭng] **28** 15

wallet [wöl/ ət] **20** 9

walnut(s) [wöl/ nət(s)] **9** 29

walrus [wöl/ rŭs] **68** 11

warm [wörm] **25** 8

索引

wash [wŏsh] **38** 16

washcloth [wŏsh′klöth′] **34** 22

washer [wŏsh′ər] **37** 40

washing machine
[wŏsh′ĭng mə shēn′] **35** 30

Washington [wŏsh′ĭng tən] **73** 47

wasp [wŏsp] **63** 20

wastepaper basket
[wāst′pā pər băs′kət] **34** 13

watch [wŏch] **23** 10

watchband [wŏch′bănd′] **23** 11

water (n) [wŏt′ər] **42** 16, **91** 30

water (v) [wŏt′ər] **26** 5

water fountain [wŏt′ər fown′tən]
87 19

water glass [wŏt′ər glăs′] **29** 6

waterfall [wŏt′ər föl] **80** 11, **89** 18

water-skier [wŏt′ər skē′ər] **59** 10

watercress [wŏt′ər krĕs′] **6** 5

watering can [wŏt′ər ĭng kăn′] **27** 16

watermelon [wŏt′ər mĕl′ən] · **9** 26

wave [wāv] **91** 24

weapon [wĕp′ənz] **48**

weather [wĕdh′ər] **25**

weather forecaster
[wĕdh′ər för′kăst ər] **86** 1

weather satellite [wĕdh′ər săt′ ə līt]
75 3

weaving [wē′vĭng] **101** 30

web [wĕb] **63** 15

wedding ring [wĕd′ĭng rĭng′] **23** 4

weights [wāts] **78** 5

west [wĕst] **71** 74

West Virginia [wĕst′ vər jĭn′ yə] **73** 48

wet [wĕt] **25** 15

wet suit [wĕt′soot′] **91** 38

whale [wāl] **68** 9

wheat [wēt] **60** 22

wheat farm [wēt′ färm′] **81**

(wheat) field [wēt′ fēld′] **81** 16

wheel [wēl] **52** 4

wheelbarrow [wēl′băr′ō] **27** 32,
82 23

wheelchair [wēl′chër′] **39** 2

whistle [wĭs′əl] **90** 5

whole [hōl] **11** 27, **79** 29

whole (chicken) [hōl′ chĭk′ən] **11** 16

width [wĭdth] **79** 35

wife [wīf] **2** 4

willow [wĭl′ō] **61** 31

wind [wĭnd] **80** 4

windbreaker [wĭnd′ brā′kər] **19** 5

windlass [wĭnd′ ləs] **58** 23

windmill [wĭnd′ mĭl′] **80** 19

window [wĭn′ dō] **27** 7, **46** 15

window cleaner [wĭn′ dō klē′ nər]
35 10

windpipe [wĭnd′ pīp′] **5** 60

windshield [wĭnd′ shēld′] **51** 45

windshield wiper [wĭnd′ shēld wī′ pər]
50 6

windsurfer [wĭnd′ sür′ fər] **59** 14

windy [wĭn′ dē] **25** 13

wine [wīn] **16** 19

wine glass [wīn′ glăs′] **29** 5

wing [wĭng] **11** 22, **57** 9, **63** 4a,
64 1a

Winter [wĭn′ tər] **26**

wipe [wīp] **38** 5

wire [wīr] **37** 35

wire mesh screen [wīr′ mĕsh skrēn′]
78 6

Wisconsin [wĭs kŏn′ sən] **73** 49

witness [wĭt′ nəs] **43** 13

witness stand [wĭt′ nəs stănd′] **43** 18

wolf [woolf] **69** 29

woman [woom′ən] **2** 1

wood [wood] **36** 4

wood plane [wood′ plān′] **37** 32

woodpecker [wood′ pĕk′ ər] **64** 17

woods [woodz] **89** 32

woodwinds [wood′ wĭndz′] **98**

wool [wool] **101** 23

word processor [würd′ prŏ′ sĕs ər]
83 7

work gloves [würk′ glŭvz′] **27** 26

workbench [würk′ bĕnch′] **36** 22

workshop [würk′ shŏp′] **36**

world [würld] **70**

worm [würm] **62** 11

wrench [rĕnch] **36** 10

wrist [rĭst] **4** 21

write [rīt] **77** 7

writer [rī′ tər] **86** 7

Wyoming [wī ō′ mĭng] **73** 50

X ray [ĕks′ rā′] **39** 1

X ray screener [ĕks′ rā skrē′ nər] **56** 11

xylophone [zī′ lə fōn′] **98** 31

yam [yăm] **7** 24

Yangtze River [yăng′ sē rĭv′ ər] **71** 69

yarn [yärn] **101** 31

Yellow Sea [yĕl′ ō sē′] **70** 37

Yenisey River [yĕn′ ə sā′ rĭv′ ər]
71 65

Yukon River [yoo′ kŏn rĭv′ ər] **71** 56

zebra [zē′ brə] **66** 18

zinnia [zĭn′ ē ə] **60** 13

zip code [zĭp′ kōd′] **46** 12

zipper [zĭp′ ər] **101** 16

zoo [zoo] **87** 1

zucchini [zoo kē′ nē] **7** 27